has built his family, his friendships, and his business has been inspirational. I believe it is important to know how someone lives, not just how they do their job. David is unique in that his emotional and relational intelligence excels as much as his financial intelligence.

This book is a solid read for anyone that wants to build a foundation or go all the way to financial independence. Some of my greatest gifts to others have been books to help them accomplish their dreams. This book will be one of them. I am ecstatic that we will all have this book as a resource! Bravo, David!"

–KEVIN BELL
Business, Finances, and Asset Development

INVEST IN YOUR LIFE,
NOT JUST YOUR PORTFOLIO

A GUIDE TO
ACHIEVING FINANCIAL INDEPENDENCE

INVEST IN YOUR

LIFE

NOT JUST YOUR PORTFOLIO

DAVID L. BLAIN, CFA

Published by Advantage, Charleston, South Carolina.
Member of Advantage Media Group.

ADVANTAGE is a registered trademark, and the Advantage colophon is a trademark of Advantage Media Group, Inc.

Printed in the United States of America.

10 9 8 7 6 5 4 3 2

ISBN: 978-1-59932-881-2
LCCN: 2019930794

Cover and layout design by Melanie Cloth.
Unless otherwise noted, all graphics in this book originated with BlueSky Wealth Advisors LLC and were designed by Melanie Cloth.

This publication is designed to provide accurate and authoritative information in regard to the subject matter covered. It is sold with the understanding that the publisher is not engaged in rendering legal, accounting, or other professional services. If legal advice or other expert assistance is required, the services of a competent professional person should be sought.

Advantage Media Group is proud to be a part of the Tree Neutral® program. Tree Neutral offsets the number of trees consumed in the production and printing of this book by taking proactive steps such as planting trees in direct proportion to the number of trees used to print books. To learn more about Tree Neutral, please visit **www.treeneutral.com.**

Advantage Media Group is a publisher of business, self-improvement, and professional development books and online learning. We help entrepreneurs, business leaders, and professionals share their Stories, Passion, and Knowledge to help others Learn & Grow. Do you have a manuscript or book idea that you would like us to consider for publishing? Please visit **advantagefamily.com** or call **1.866.775.1696.**

*To my awesome wife, Caroline, who is my inspiration,
and to my Mom and Dad for the personal values and
principles of finance they instilled in me at an early age.*

TABLE OF CONTENTS

PART FIVE: CREATE A LEGACY YOU LOVE

DOING SOMETHING DIFFERENT

Growing up in the Washington, DC, region, I often took city transit home from high school. As I watched the commuters jostling on the crowded buses, I understood the meaning of "the rat race." I *wanted* something different than that for myself, and so I figured I'd have to do something different.

Every workday for four decades, my father Paul, a budget analyst, steadfastly reported to his job at the US Department of Defense. He worked hard to support his family and, in many ways, is my hero. But despite his being successful in creating a decent life for us, I knew I wanted something different.

I wanted more excitement in life!

My mother Marie's career came closer to the action I craved. A registered nurse, she took several years off when my sister and brother and I were little before later working in a doctor's office. She made sure we got a good head start with deep Christian values. My parents sacrificed a lot to uphold their values and their faith, including sending me to a Catholic high school—Bishop Ireton—in Alexandria, Virginia.

My father also taught us the meaning of money—that it must serve a purpose that goes beyond instant gratification. He taught us the fundamental wisdom of spending less than we earn and setting aside money for the future. Conservative by nature, he bought our cars in cash with the savings bonds purchased through his government payroll.

MY TURN TO SERVE AND LEAD

I was born in 1966 during the thick of the Vietnam War, and I heard a lot about the conflict while growing up. Through many of my parents' friends and neighbors in the military, I developed a deep respect for our armed forces and their mission. A young history buff, I spent time at the public library and became aware that many people who didn't have a heart for the mission had been sent to war. Even many of the leaders lacked conviction. How can a nation expect to prevail when people who don't want to be there are leading others who don't want to be there?

I resolved that, when my turn to serve came, I'd be in charge. And by being in the military, I hoped to maybe do some good.

So, after graduating early from high school, I went off to Notre Dame on an ROTC scholarship while waiting for an appointment to West Point. As a freshman, I enjoyed the military maneuvers we conducted in ROTC—the mock battles and ambushes and even assault missions that featured rappelling out of helicopters. I seldom went to classes; I must have figured that my brilliant big sister attending Notre Dame a year ahead of me was getting good enough grades for both of us!

Nonetheless, through Senator Warren of Virginia and acceptance by West Point, I got an appointment to this prestigious military school. There, I dove into my studies and responsibilities, eventually graduating as a Distinguished Honor Graduate.

At first, I aspired to become a pilot but was persuaded to go into the US Army Infantry and Rangers where, I was told, I'd have the greatest impact as a leader. I attended the US Army Airborne School in Fort Benning and got my wings, then spent the summer of 1987 at the Fulda Gap in Germany with the 11th Armored Cavalry Regiment.

My high class ranking at West Point allowed me options as to where and how I would serve. I chose the infantry so I could become a US Army Ranger, and I chose Fort Bragg where the 82nd Airborne Division was based.

I approached going to US Army Ranger School as a way to strengthen me and make me better able to serve. In my unit, I volunteered to march straight into the danger zone and tackle whatever challenges came my way—always preceded by painstaking preparation. As a rapid response unit, the 82nd Division was often deployed quickly to trouble spots—where the action and excitement would be.

A DIFFERENT KIND OF SERVICE

During my military career, I was also an enthusiastic investor, so a 1999 career change to financial planning came naturally. Themes from my military years carried through into my financial services career, including thorough preparation and a dedication to serving others. Through all those years, I have maintained an adventurous spirit imbued with deep values that came from the quality of my upbringing. My parents shaped me well and for that I'm forever grateful.

During my years of service in financial planning, I've met many people in need of solid financial guidance. Often, they're thriving in their careers but are unsure how to turn their hard-earned income into wealth. They seek reassurance they'll be able to retire comfortably, and they know they need to be prepared financially, but how?

With a barrage of information and conflicting advice on financial topics, they wonder which "advisors" are truly on their side and not primarily interested in lining their own pockets.

> **Themes from my military years carried through into my financial services career, including thorough preparation and a dedication to serving others.**

As their financial situations get more complicated, they feel apprehensive. Many are unsure of what they want to accomplish in life, so when contemplating their future, they feel more stress than excitement.

If this describes you, you're not alone. In my two decades of practice, I've helped hundreds of people gain control of their destinies and attain financial freedom. We have worked together to:

- Develop better financial habits to achieve meaningful things in the world.

- Set a course to realize their dreams and even share part with less fortunate people.

- Put in place strategies to prepare for unforeseen fiscal emergencies.

If that's what you seek, this book will be your guide.

WHAT TO EXPECT FROM THIS BOOK

Perhaps you picked up this book for specific tips on where to invest your money. However, for the most part, your investment decisions depend on your circumstances and priorities. That means a good strategy for one investor could be disastrous for another.

Let me reassure you that I understand the problems you face. Although I was successful in my military career and had a good start as an investor, I still felt unsure of the next steps to take, the proper strategies to follow, or the people I should trust with my finances. (You'll read about that in the Introduction.) As those questions loomed large, I began an odyssey to acquire a thorough financial education. Doing so led me to establish a fee-only advisory firm, BlueSky Wealth Advisors, that I still lead today.

Consider this book to be a survey of the wisdom I've gained through my education and two decades of experience as a professional advisor. As I share my experiences, good and bad, I'll also introduce you to a variety of lessons learned through my clients.

I invite you to come with me on a financial journey through these chapters. Along the way, remember this: if you *want* something different, you must *do* something different. Let's discover what this means for your portfolio and your life!

SAVING LIVELIHOODS

A s an army infantry officer in Iraq in the early 1990s, I saw events during the Desert Storm campaign I can never forget. However, few experiences have influenced me as much as what I encountered years later while on the slopes of Mount Rainier. There, I met a deadly force that ultimately changed the course of my career and my life.

In 1990, I was a young man eager to take on any challenge. I had endured intense qualifying training to become a US Army Ranger, and I had given it my all. I had also seen what happened to my peers who messed up or couldn't take it. They didn't make it.

No way would I quit or even show myself vulnerable to getting injured. For example, in the US Army Ranger School, I broke my foot during a paratroop exercise and still marched through the desert in Utah with a broken foot. Ever since my time at West Point, the lessons had been clear: Don't complain. Watch out for your buddy's back. Trust that someone else will watch out for yours.

My first duty assignment after US Army Ranger training was at Fort Bragg, North Carolina, with the 504th Parachute Infantry Regiment of the 82nd Airborne Division. I showed up as a brand-new second lieutenant early in 1990, just after the unit returned from the invasion of Panama that had deposed the dictator Manuel Noriega. When the Iraqi forces of Saddam Hussein invaded Kuwait in 1990, the 82nd Division was sent to secure the Saudi Arabia border in the

Gulf War. We stayed there about a year during the build-up of troops, the air war, and the ground war before returning to the United States in mid-1991.

Once I got back, I tried out for the elite 75th Ranger Regiment, was chosen for the 2nd Battalion, and headed out to my assignment at Fort Lewis near Tacoma, Washington. I was proud to be part of the same battalion that, on D-Day in World War II, had scaled the hundred-foot cliffs at Normandy with rope ladders and grapples to knock out the German guns at Pointe du Hoc. As part of our training, we spent time with the SAS in Britain. There, the rigorous training included getting pummeled with water from a fire hose during POW escape-and-recapture maneuvers outdoors in Scotland in the middle of winter!

On my next major mission, I was bound for Somalia to join the supposed peacekeeping and humanitarian initiative, Operation Restore Hope. The summer before our deployment, I set out to climb Mount Rainier—*an exciting accomplishment worthy of a US Army Ranger,* I thought. After reaching the summit, I made my way back down to my pickup truck and pulled out onto the mountain road to head home.

SUDDENLY MY WORLD CHANGED

My training at West Point and with the Rangers had prepared me to face the elemental struggles of man against nature and the indignities and atrocities of man against man. But nothing had addressed the monumental challenge that pitted man against elk.

One moment I was cruising along; the next I was wildly swerving to avoid striking an elk crossing the road—a beast as big as my truck. My vehicle careened off the road and flipped onto its roof in the ditch. I kicked out the back window and crawled out of it to hike to the nearest farmhouse a mile away. There, I called the police for assistance. By the time we got back to my truck, somebody had stolen all my hiking gear and my wallet, too, which I'd left on the console. Without it, I couldn't even prove my identity.

In the years ahead, my whole body ached, and I had lost feeling and strength in my right arm. I toughed it out because I couldn't admit to anyone, including myself, that I was injured and in pain. Duty called me to Somalia. My unit was not part of the forces that faced heavy fighting in Mogadishu. Instead, we remained at the staging area rehearsing our mission. As much as I wanted to be where the action was, due to my injuries, I had trouble carrying my rucksack, aiming a rifle, and wearing a parachute. I knew I was fortunate to stay put.

Following the Somalia mission, I was sent to the Infantry Officers Advanced Course at Fort Benning in Georgia. After graduating, I was selected to attend the Special Forces Assessment and Selection Course at Fort Bragg, North Carolina. This course turned out to be another three weeks of physical and psychological hell. I managed to make it through and was chosen to attend the full Special Forces Qualification Course, even though, by then, I could barely use my right arm. After a short while in the "Q" course, I finally saw a doctor who noted considerable damage to vertebrae in my upper spine. My rendezvous with the elk had left me with serious neck problems.

In late 1994, I was chosen to fill an opening for an officer with US Army Ranger Regiment experience in the US Army Special Operations Command. For the next five years at Fort Bragg, I held various positions within the special operation community. My operational experiences ranged from Bosnia in the European theater to Iraq and Liberia in the Middle Eastern theater. My final position was that of company commander at the US John F. Kennedy Special Warfare Center and School.

During those years, I regained most of the use of my arm. Also, an MRI showed remarkable improvement in the condition of my vertebrae—to the point of not needing the recommended spinal fusion. Still, my physical issues destined me to a desk job with Special Ops rather than doing what I loved—experiencing the excitement of being in the field with the troops.

While my neck injury was slowing me down, the prospect of family obligations was giving me pause. I had to redefine myself.

FAREWELL TO THE ARMY, HELLO TO LOVE

So began my metamorphosis from a soldier to a financial planner/advisor. That might seem a radical change of pace, but today, working with my financial planning clients, I relive these familiar themes learned in the military:

- Set your sights on clear goals and pursue them diligently.

- Be prepared for everything and anything.

- Get in shape to face the big risks out there.

- Surround yourself with people you can trust.

- Understand your limits but never limit your potential.

- Do it right—and do what's right.

Something else happened that forever changed my trajectory. Not long after meeting the elk on that lonely mountain road, I had a greater life-altering experience. I fell in love.

I had met Caroline while I was stationed at Fort Lewis. This Georgia girl was in Seattle to pursue her graduate studies at the University of Washington. A couple of friends at West Point had gone to high school with her in Atlanta and introduced us in Washington. Caroline and I met socially, but we didn't date then; she had a boyfriend at the time. Yet even though she returned to Georgia to begin her teaching career, I never forgot about her.

When my military career brought me to Fort Benning not far from where Caroline was teaching, I looked her up right away. We met for a date in Atlanta, and then I invited her down to check out Fort Benning. On the day she was to visit, she arrived earlier than I expected. She had to wait a few hours until I finally showed up, sweating under the weight of a heavy backpack. "I was out training," I explained to her. "I had spare time, so I started getting ready for the special forces training I'll be doing up at Fort Bragg."

Caroline's expression seemed partly bemused, party amused. "On my way down here from Atlanta," she later told me, "I saw this crazy guy along the road, twenty miles out in the middle of nowhere, lugging a huge backpack. So that was you?" I confessed that, yes, that crazy guy was me. Not so crazy by US Army Rangers standards, though. That's what Rangers do in their free time. They work out; they run; they go to the gym; they prepare to become prepared.

As our relationship deepened, Caroline took a teaching job in a town about thirty miles from Fort Bragg so we could continue our courtship. We knew by then we had something special, but our values prevented us from moving in together. Before long, I asked her to be my wife, and we married in 1995.

Besides the neck issues I dealt with constantly during that phase, it was not lost on me that the divorce rate among soldiers in US Army Special Operations was something like 90 percent. I vowed my marriage and family life would come first. I knew I had served well, and I felt called to serve in another way.

So, before the turn of the millennium, I said farewell to the military after a decade as a US Army Ranger and Special Operations soldier. I received an honorable medical discharge. Miraculously, it would be nearly fifteen years before I would need surgery to replace my three crushed vertebrae.

INVESTING IN MY FUTURE

But then what? I looked back on my life for clues as to where I'd best fit in. Who and what had shaped me? I needed to better understand myself, so I could gain a clear picture of what I'd be doing for the rest of my life. *What was David Blain meant to be?*

In my middle-class household, my parents were not wealthy, but they were certainly rich in the values they passed on to their children. I was taught to always be honest, work hard, spend frugally, and save for the future. Toward that end, I learned the basics of investing. I also learned to be an entrepreneur.

My entrepreneurial bent had come at a young age. Every morning, I got up in the dark to deliver *The Washington Post,* and I mowed lawns in the afternoons and on weekends. With a friend, I started a bicycle recycling business. After we finished our paper routes, we'd collect old bikes left at the curb with the trash. Then, in my buddy's garage, we disassembled them, built new bicycles from the parts, and sold them for a nice profit. We did the same with discarded lawnmowers. What a good income for a teenager! Dad took me to the local bank to invest in certificates of deposit that, at the time, were yielding remarkable 14 and 15 percent returns. The concept of using my money to make more money captivated me.

I continued working and dabbling in investments until I went away to the University of Notre Dame and then to West Point. There, in addition to math, science, and engineering, I took an elective on finance and investment. It was taught by a brilliant army major with an MBA from Harvard who, at the age of thirty-something, had achieved financial freedom. He motivated me to begin investing in earnest.

After graduating in 1989, my military career progressed nicely—and so did my portfolio. I did well with stocks and bonds and branched out into real estate. As my investment earnings grew to nearly as much as my army pay, I sought out a professional advisor. I had hired a CPA to help with my taxes, but I needed an advisor who could do more than fill out my tax forms. I wanted advice on reaching my long-term goal of financial independence and minimizing the amount of tax I had to pay.

What I found was that most "advisors" just wanted to sell something. One firm "specializing in the planning needs of military officers" invited us to seminars where, over a free dinner, we heard a pitch for life insurance. *I'm single and I don't need life insurance,* I thought, and these folks want me to buy tons of it. The firm also peddled mutual funds to earn a 50 percent commission during the first year.

I found those practices to be egregious. As a result, I developed a distrust not only of that firm but of the wider industry and the types of advisors out there. I concluded that, if I wanted to invest confidently, I would need to invest in myself. I made it my mission to develop expertise in financial matters. Before long, my peers were asking me for tips on investing and taxes as their informal financial advisor.

Seeing my military career wind down, an acquaintance suggested I become a financial advisor at the firm where he worked, a large national stock brokerage. My expression must have let him know what I was thinking: *No way! I don't want to sell stuff to people!*

"It's not like that," he assured me. "It's like running your own business, and we do actual planning to help people. It's not all about selling our products."

However, I found out otherwise. I joined the firm's training program, and by the end of the first week I had my assignments: write down the names and phone numbers of at least a hundred people I knew and cold-call them. When I had finished that, I was expected to go door-to-door in my neighborhood. Nope. Not the job for me. After the third week, I moved on. Next, I got interested in working for a so-called planner who turned out to be little more than an annuity salesman. Again, I moved on.

While wrapping up my final days in US Army Special Operations, I attended a conference of the National Association of Personal Financial Advisors (NAPFA). There, *I felt as if I'd finally met my people.* These professionals were truly helping their clients. They had no interest in making sales pitches. In fact, NAPFA members weren't allowed to even have a securities license to sell products. They were committed to the fiduciary standard and true financial planning.

These planners were doing what I wanted to do—serving others honorably and treating people as I wanted to be treated. *Finally, I was not alone in my values.* The public wanted what I had to offer, and NAPFA provided the inspiration I needed to start my new career.

EVOLUTION OF BLUESKY WEALTH ADVISORS

To do things my way, I concluded, I'd need to go back to my entre-preneurial roots. So, that year—1999—I launched my financial advisory and investment practice, initially named Blain Investment Counsel and later, DL Blain & Co. I settled on the name BlueSky Wealth Advisors in 2013.

To qualify as a NAPFA member, I had to take a fiduciary oath, submit a financial plan for peer review, and have my business practices examined for any conflict of interest. It was exciting to become a part of this dedicated but small group—only 500 nationwide at the time—that wanted to change the way financial advice is delivered.

At first, I charged a percentage of assets under management, a traditional fee structure. Originally, my focus was on helping people with their investments, but I saw how seriously people needed good advice and assistance in areas where I could add value. Meanwhile, I moved toward a planning fee in combination with the percentage of assets. A decade or so later, I went to a flat fee.

That evolution just made sense. BlueSky Wealth Advisors helps people in both their accumulation and distribution stages of life. Older clients with significant wealth have uncomplicated needs and take relatively little of our time, while young professionals with small portfolios need help with exceedingly complex business and family needs. I concluded that the best way to charge people was based on the complexity of their situation and not the size of their portfolio. Why? Because it doesn't take ten times the effort to manage $5,000,000 as it does to manage $500,000. We have since refined the algorithm for our fee, tailoring it to each client's personal and financial situation, specific requirements, and choice of services. Under traditional models, BlueSky could collect more fees from some of our clients than we do. That doesn't mean we should.

Day after day and year after year, I advise clients to pursue the goals that are meaningful to them. Otherwise, what's the point of financial planning? Having a vision and a mission in your life and career brings real purpose to your money. Conversely, having a fortune without a focus defeats the purpose of building wealth.

In my own life and career, I strive to put my values into practice and to do what is right and what is fair. My colleagues at BlueSky share that ideal. We are committed to providing high-quality advice free of conflicts so we can serve people with their routine matters or their biggest challenges. We help families recognize and deal with dangers that could put them inches away from devastation if we're not careful. To be fearless without regard to consequences would be foolhardy. Forgive the cliché, but it is true: discretion is the better part of valor.

SAVING LIVELIHOODS INSTEAD OF LIVES

I take seriously the trust families have placed in BlueSky to help shape their futures. They believe in my leadership and depend on me, and I must never let them down. I am still a soldier. I know that, but ultimately, those I serve will be the judge.

Together, we must constantly review the plan, survey the landscape, scan the horizon, and look for anything that is out of place or missing as we keep moving ever onward. Doing it right is still a huge responsibility, and so is doing what is right.

PART ONE

. . .

DO YOU KNOW WHERE YOU'RE GOING?

Success is measured by much more than a big portfolio. Your money should serve a purpose—to support the values you wish to pass on and the dreams you hold in your heart. Before deciding on any investments, identify why you wish to attain financial independence. What principles guide you? What goals do you hope to reach?

As you set out on your journey, do you know where you're going?

CHAPTER 1

LIFE ISN'T A PORTFOLIO

The steps to financial independence are not that difficult to grasp. What is harder is identifying your destination and dedicating yourself to reaching it. No fortune will make you happy if you fail to dream—or if your dreams fail.

W hen we met, Caroline was studying for her graduate degree in education. When we began courting seriously, she was teaching middle school. A year later, she was losing faith in the educational system and her ability to influence the lives of kids amid the chaos of crowded classrooms. She concluded that there must be something more than that to pursue as a career.

We were also contemplating how we would educate our own children, and we knew upfront that it was not going to be in the public schools. Nor would it be in the traditional Catholic school system, which had changed so much over the years. We did, however, want a Catholic education for our kids. We hoped to infuse our deep-seated values in them, and we wanted to shape their attitudes and behaviors free of the sort of negative influences that young people so often pick up from their peers.

We married in 1995, but it was five years before we had children. Paul led the way, followed by Olivia, James, Patrick, and Kathleen in the ensuing decade. By the time the first arrived, however, Caroline had everything in place. Well in advance, she had done the research, attended homeschool groups, and narrowed the options. We decided on a program called the Seton Home Study School, and Caroline rose to the challenge of becoming the full-time teacher for our family. Her undergraduate degree is in English and art—she is a fabulous artist, and a variety of her works hang in my office building—but she teaches the full range of disciplines to our children. All five have thrived under her tutelage.

I deeply appreciate her sacrifice. Caroline chose the betterment of our family as her career until our children all graduated from high school. She might have continued to teach in the school system, perhaps rising in the administrative ranks and drawing a sizable income on our behalf, but she chose to contribute something more meaningful than money. We set a goal that reflected our values and what really mattered to our family. Caroline invested in us. To give of herself was the higher calling.

The Best Things in Life . . .

We often hear that the best things in life are free. In truth, many of life's best things come at a price. We often must sacrifice to attain a greater good.

To be true to your values isn't necessarily easy. You may need to give up some things along the way, but if you start investing early in your dreams, you are more likely to reach them.

Through the years, as I have begun relationships with new clients, I have often clearly seen they are not enjoying their so-called successful careers. They want more in life than just working day after day for their paycheck, even though it is a large one. I hear a refrain that goes like this: "I went to school, got my degree, did the things I was supposed to do. And I guess I'm a success—right? Everyone says so. But I'm not happy, David. I'm so busy making money and paying for everything I'm supposed to have that I can't stop to think anymore." They are making plenty of income, but they also are juggling mortgages and bills and taxes and paying off their student loans while saving for their children's tuition, not to mention trying to set aside something for retirement. They feel far from financially free. They feel trapped.

Colleen was one such person. When she came to see me, she appeared to have it all: a successful career with a Fortune 500 company, lots of money in her retirement plan at work, a fine house and nice cars, and a significant stock portfolio awarded to her by her company. Inside, though, she wasn't happy. She felt

> **I hear a refrain that goes like this: "I went to school, got my degree, did the things I was supposed to do. And I guess I'm a success—right? Everyone says so. But I'm not happy.**

conflicted and anxious but didn't know how to fix it. She knew she needed to change something but couldn't figure out what it was.

Since her divorce, Colleen had been working furiously to raise her family and send her children to college. She was trying to do all the right things, but she had not focused on the big picture of what she wanted out of life. She was jaded from her experiences with financial salespeople and remained skeptical about how much an advisor could help her. One of her sons recommended that she visit a fee-only advisor who deals with a range of planning issues.

As we began our relationship, I certainly needed to know all the details of her finances, but more important, I needed to know more about her. I soon discovered that what she valued most was not the money, in and of itself, but rather what money could do to create a better life for her and her family. She wanted financial independence so she could spend time with her kids and her soon-to-be-born grandchildren. Colleen's life was a swirl. She was in tears during our first meeting. One might think that she was the picture of success, that she had it made, but that wasn't how she felt. What she truly wanted was a satisfying family life.

Colleen's fundamental problem was that she didn't know how to make her money become a means toward that end. She was losing sight of how to enjoy life. She could afford to pursue dreams and didn't need to keep working at a career she wasn't enjoying, but she couldn't wrap her head around the concept of not having an income from a job. She wanted to be responsible, and was clearly adept at corporate finance, but personal finance is a different matter.

It's not about showing the best possible quarterly earnings. It's about achieving what's important to you.

What, then, were her objectives? She told me she had long dreamed of buying a beach house where her extended family could gather, but she didn't know whether she could afford to do so. Over the next several months, we designed a plan for her to realize that dream. She developed the confidence to make an offer on a beach house, and we walked her through the steps of the purchase. This was not so much a real estate investment as it was an investment in family. We also put her on track to step down from her job by age sixty so she would have much more time to spend with her loved ones.

By defining her goals and taking steps toward reaching them, Colleen removed much of the stress from her life. You could see it in her smile. Because she was focusing on what she truly wanted to achieve, she was happier. Her distress had come from not knowing where she was going in life. The big picture was escaping her. She needed to get a grasp on what truly mattered to her and pursue it with the help of the right kind of leadership—and that doesn't mean financial salespeople. I helped her see what she was having trouble seeing herself. *Success was not measured by her money. Success came from knowing where her money could take her.* Colleen discovered *why* she had a portfolio.

Financial Independence

You probably know people who are making fabulous incomes but, nonetheless, are living from paycheck to paycheck. A husband and wife in Silicon Valley, for example, might be making $500,000 a year between them, yet not understand why they are broke. I have come across a lot of such people. They have become successful as measured by their income, but they have not achieved financial security. I want to help such people break free of those chains.

A central goal for most people is to attain a degree of financial independence. Generally, they get there by setting aside some of each paycheck and putting that money to work generating an income on its own. When that passive income exceeds living expenses, the investor is well on the way to financial freedom.

How do you know when you reach that point? It depends on your needs and expectations. Some people require little and live modestly. Others have built a lifestyle that requires hundreds of thousands of dollars a year.

Few rules apply to everyone. When people come to see me, they often have a lot of specific questions. "Is this a good stock to buy?" or "Will I be able to deduct this from my taxes?" or "Is this the right time to invest in bonds?" Questions such as those are important, but I realized early in my career that other questions should come first. I need to know certain things about new clients before we can jump into the numbers. For example:

- What are they trying to accomplish in the long term?

- How much are they willing and able to accept immediately?

- How soon might they need the money they are thinking of investing that way?

The hardest part about designing a portfolio is not choosing investments; it is about matching them to the portfolio owner's personality.

The client's personal and family situation, as well as temperament and tolerance for risk, will have much to do with how and where and when to invest. Sometimes the answer that might seem to make the most sense is not the right one for the individual. For example, people on the cusp of retirement often wonder whether they should pay off the mortgage. You could go solely by the numbers to make that decision, but so much else comes into play. What are your other objectives? How important to you is paying off that debt? Some people want to continue receiving the tax break and figure they are better off investing that money elsewhere rather than sinking it into the house. To other people, however, paying off the mortgage is a meaningful and symbolic accomplishment. They feel like a winner. Such a deeply held belief cannot be ignored.

A Portfolio with Purpose

Once you have reached the point of financial independence, your attention can turn to something besides building that portfolio. You can focus more on fulfillment. Life becomes less about making money and more about what your money can do, and that gets personal. It comes down to honoring a value or a higher purpose that you hold dear. For many, the tricky part is figuring out what that is. We want to make sure that you are on a path to achieve something in life that you want. Your money should support your values and goals.

Ask yourself why you have been plugging away all these years. Most of us in the developed world do not worry about access to food, clean water, or shelter. Though the basics of life do come at an expense, it doesn't take a lot of money in modern society to maintain an existence. But who wants to just exist? Having attained financial independence, you finally have more freedom to engage in a meaningful secondary "career," a philanthropic one, perhaps, or an educational pursuit. Your heart's desire awaits you.

Though they seek financial independence, many people have trouble adjusting to it. They can't get off the hamster wheel. I have often observed people spending an inordinate amount of time organizing and tracking their investment accounts, insurance policies, and taxes. Organization and monitoring are good, of course, within reason. I have met people, though, who are so busy making money and managing it that they aren't taking enough time to enjoy life.

A delightful couple, Darrell and Donna, once came in to see me to start planning for their retirement. They had worked hard in successful careers and figured it was high time to relax—if they could find the hours in the day to do so. "We want to travel," Darrell said, "and do a lot of scuba diving—but what I really want to do is enjoy my boat more. That's my dream." Donna struggled to hold her tongue and then began to laugh. "Ah, yes, the boat!" she said. "You bought that thing three years ago, and we haven't been out on it once!" She was only pretending to chide him, and Darrell grinned broadly. "Well," he said, "I guess it's time we stop spending so much time succeeding so we can get around to living."

I have walked with many such folks as they took the steps toward financial independence. In this book, I hope to guide you along your path, too. I can share with you the wisdom, facts, and concrete measures I know have worked for many others. I can show you how to build your portfolio to attain financial freedom, but what I cannot tell you is what to do with it once you get it. That is up to you to decide.

Consider this: If you are not pursuing what matters to you, will you be truly happy that your investments have soared? Is that success? Financial independence is a worthy goal, but what do you intend to do with your good fortune? Money does matter, and we will be exploring many ways you can make the most of it. However, the ultimate way to make the most of it is to put it toward the uses that reflect your values and goals.

> **I can show you how to build your portfolio to attain financial freedom, but what I cannot tell you is what to do with it once you get it. That is up to you to decide.**

A portfolio with purpose is a rich one indeed.

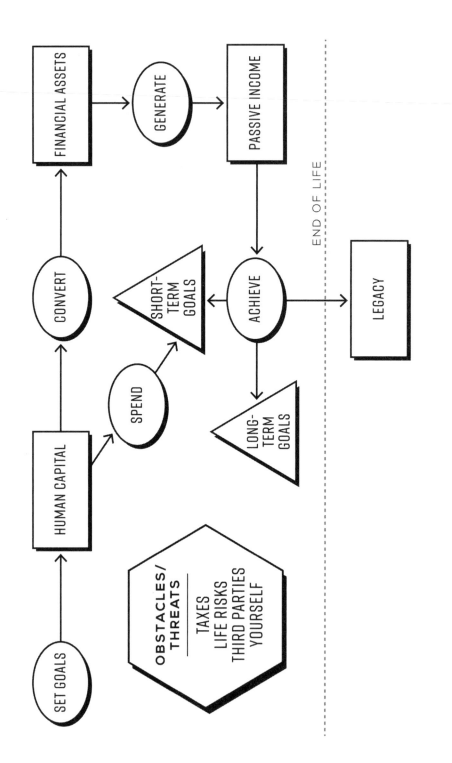

The steps toward reaching financial independence, which I have been advocating for years, are not complicated. Here is a summary with a chart to illustrate them. You will learn more about these steps in the chapters to come.

- **Set goals.** They can be simple or grand, but just get started. Define your objectives, both short and long term.

- **Earn a living.** Trade your time and your labor (which we call "human capital") for compensation.

- **Fund the short-term goals.** You will need to use some of your current earnings to sustain yourself and your family. Your expenses will include food, shelter, and educational fees, for example.

- **Defer consumption and save.** The key to attaining financial independence is to take part of your earnings and set them aside for the future.

- **Convert to financial capital.** Don't just stuff those savings into a mattress. Invest in things that don't require your time, effort, and talent, such as stocks, bonds, and real estate.

- **Create passive income.** Don't spend excessively. Allow your financial assets to multiply and generate passive income.

- **Achieve longer-term goals.** As your passive income grows, you gain the ability to accomplish more of your longer-term objectives.

- **Mitigate threats.** Take steps to reduce the impact of several significant challenges to your ability to become financially independent.

- **Leave a legacy.** Depending on your goals, the cycle of passive income generation can continue after you are gone. You can leave a legacy for your family or other purposes.

CHAPTER 2

DECIDING YOUR DESTINATION

Once you are clear about your values, you can set specific goals that support what is meaningful to you and your family. You should decide when you wish to accomplish those goals. Then calculate the cost of attaining them. That way, you will know clearly when you have reached your destination.

s soldiers in Iraq, we knew the mission. We didn't hear all the details of the news cycle, but we had no doubt why US troops were there: our job was to get Saddam Hussein out of Kuwait and guard against any other aggressions he might undertake in the region. Our confidence that the mission was in place helped us make sense of our day-to-day duties.

By the mid-1990s when the United States sent troops to Bosnia, attitudes were changing. In those "peacekeeping mission" years, the military seemed to be less of a national priority. Because of those shifting sands of policy in the Clinton era, a lot of servicemen and servicewomen started to lose faith in the military's mission. They had trouble seeing the point of what they were doing. Ultimately, disillusionment drove many people away from the military.

Traditionally, the typical American soldier wants to know the *why*. Once American soldiers believe in the mission, they will go to the ends of the earth to do it right. By contrast, we found it hard to find anyone in the Iraqi army who wanted to be in charge. The Iraqis didn't even seem to know what that meant. Their mind-set was to obey the orders, not to issue them.

When the United States pulls out of trouble spots, the buildup of domestic forces often goes slowly because running the show is not necessarily the ambition of the locals. American soldiers, by contrast, want to assume the leadership roles. They want the opportunity to be in charge—that is, as long as the mission isn't murky and they can grasp the rationale.

As a financial planner, I have found that a murky mission also tends to stifle the ambitions of my clients. They want to see the big picture we are striving to accomplish. They want to envision the results of all their sacrifices and what they stand to gain if they step up to the challenge. And as they take charge of their finances, they want leadership they can trust.

> **Once you recognize your goals in life, you will be likely to take the steps to reach them. When you know the mission, the sacrifices seem worthwhile.**

Once you recognize your goals in life, you will be likely to take the steps to reach them. When you know the mission, the sacrifices seem worthwhile. That doesn't mean you need to understand all the intricate details of financial management. Instead, you need to align yourself with someone who does, someone you trust. Generally, people who are not full-time finance professionals lack that expertise and prefer to delegate the task to professionals.

"Are We There Yet?"

Most parents at some point hear this question coming from the back seat of the family car, perhaps during a long drive to a vacation spot: "Are we there yet?" The kids feel a sense of impatience and anxiety because they don't know how the trip has been mapped out. They anticipate the destination with excitement but also with apprehension. Because they don't know what it takes to get there, they feel uneasy about whether and when they will arrive.

Not knowing is stressful. In the US Army Ranger school and the Special Forces Assessment and Selection course, we hardly ever knew how long, how far, or where we were going. That's psychologically tough for most people, and we were put to the test during training to ensure we wouldn't break in warfare.

In their financial journey, grownups often feel like the kids in the back seat. One of the most common questions that people ask (particularly when they are contemplating retirement) is whether they are there yet. They are excited about getting to the destination, but often they are in the dark about the details. Often, they are unclear about where "there" is. After decades of work, they are eager to move on to the next stage of life, whatever that may be. To many, it's a great unknown.

Knowing the big plan greatly helps. You can begin to develop a sense of direction and set concrete goals by asking yourself thought-provoking questions such as these:

- What are my basic needs, wants, and desires?

- If I didn't have to work all day, what would I do with my time?

- What will most fulfill me?

- What do I want to accomplish in life?

- What do I value?

Setting goals comes easily for some people. For others, it is difficult, particularly when it comes to envisioning longer-term goals. Caroline can attest to that as she homeschools our five children. Many days, her long-term goal is simply to finish the schoolwork, put some good food on the table, and make it through the day with all the children still alive. When you have countless daily tasks in front of you competing for your attention, it can be harder to visualize the future.

Identify Your Core Values

Though it might feel overwhelming to try to list a bunch of goals, an easy way to start is to identify what you value. That will make it much easier to set some goals. It's important to find the words that express those values. Either verbalize them, or, even better, write them down. What fulfills you? What do you enjoy doing? For example, if you value a good education, then a natural goal might be to establish college funds for your children. As in my family's case, you might choose the homeschool route early on.

Financial freedom depends on your ability to save and to defer consumption. You must plan. You must take the time to sit down and figure out what you value, where you want to be, and why. When you have that vision, you will be able to resist temptations that do not support it. You can say, "I'm not going to buy that shiny new Tesla with my latest stock grant. I'm going to drive my own car for a few more years and put that $100,000 into my portfolio for the future." The first step to financial independence is to take the time to come up with a plan that supports your values.

Among my first clients were Robert and Doris, who were in their mid-forties when I met them. I would drive to their home to work with them. He was a project manager with a large technology firm, and she was self-employed. I soon learned how important their family was to them. We brainstormed to establish some goals—short-term, intermediate, and long-term—that in some way supported that core value.

> **Financial freedom depends on your ability to save and to defer consumption. You must plan. You must take the time to sit down and figure out what you value, where you want to be, and why.**

Among those goals were moving to a new house, taking an overseas family vacation each year, and putting their two children through college. We met those objectives through a savings and investment strategy. We laddered their term insurance to cover their risks as their portfolio grew until it reached the point where they didn't need insurance anymore. That means we set up several term policies that expired at predetermined times as the family's need for insurance lessened. Doris returned to work when the kids were older, and we put virtually all her income into an individual 401(k) plan.

Today, Robert and Doris are in their early sixties. The children are out on their own now, and my firm has been working with them, too, on their own journeys to independence. I remember when they were little kids playing in the yard. Today, they are young adults who are well on their way to achieving their goals.

All those years ago, when I met Robert and Doris, they lacked a sense of direction: What was the point of all their hard work? As a project manager, though, Robert understood the importance of planning and designing. As a first step, we crystallized their core value in writing. Putting it in words made it palpable. They then could focus on what they specifically needed to do to support their sense of family. Each decision they weighed against their statement of values.

With the principle of bonding as a family in mind, they did more than save and invest for their tomorrows; they also attended to their todays, taking major family vacations—an African safari, for example, and a trip through Europe, with more to come. As a rule, however, they made frugal choices such as driving ten-year-old cars.

Recently, the couple reached another milestone: both were able to quit their full-time jobs at age sixty-one. Their sacrifice and discipline and careful planning paid off. They have more precious time to devote to family, and now, they are happy grandparents. Robert and Doris are living their values.

Helping people identify their dreams and set their goals is the most gratifying aspect of what I do. I get to work with people during the excitement of their anticipation. I am with them on their quest, and the pursuit of happiness is often more fulfilling than the happiness itself. Think of it this way: Are kids more excited before they open their Christmas presents than afterward?

The Goal-Setting Process

The goal-setting process is straightforward but not easy. First, determine what you value most. Then ascertain those specific near-term and long-term goals that support what you value or fulfill a basic need. Put a date on each of the goals along with what it would cost to live that kind of life or achieve those types of goals. Do a little more math and decide what you need to do today in terms of savings or rate of return to make each goal a reality on whatever date you selected.

A goal is not a goal unless there's a date and a dollar amount on it. You can say, "I'd like to go to the moon someday," but that's not a goal. A goal would be phrased like this: "By the time I'm sixty-five, SpaceX will be taking people to the moon for around $1 million, so I'll save X dollars a month today so I can be one of them." When you put a date and cost to an objective, you have set a goal.

To place a monetary value on a goal isn't saying the money matters more. Rather, we acknowledge that society runs on money. If you go to the grocery store, you won't be able to buy anything with the goodness in your heart. You can't pay with kindness; you need to hand over money. Nothing is wrong with setting monetary goals to pay for what you wish to achieve. Money, as they say, makes the world go 'round.

Once you set a goal and make a plan to pay for it, you gain confidence to act on that plan. *That is how you succeed.* You might desire to achieve something lofty, but without a plan in place, you never will muster the confidence to make it happen. You will end up doing nothing.

Planning leads to confidence, which leads to action, which leads to success. After you figure out what you truly value, then you will work hard to achieve it.

THE THREE-STEP GOAL-SETTING PROCESS	
1	Determine what you value or need.
2	Set specific short-term and long-term goals with dates.
3	Calculate the cost needed to achieve those goals.

The Magic of Writing It Down

When I was a new cadet at West Point, the accommodations were austere. Each of us had a steel-framed bed, mattress, and pillow. We each had a wardrobe, in which our clothes had to be folded just so. We were given a basic metal desk with a chair and a bookshelf. As plebes, we each were allowed one personal framed photo. That was it.

On our desks, we were required to post a 3 x 5 card on which we had to write three things we intended to accomplish. I remember looking at my card every day because, after all, there wasn't much else to look at in my room.

Life in a military academy consisted of three disciplines: academics, physical fitness, and military leadership. Your class rank was a composite of how well you did in each. If you were in the top 5 percent of your class, you got gold stars on your collar. One of my three goals was to remain a "star man" every semester. It was worse to lose your stars than to never get them in the first place.

Another goal was to excel in physical fitness by scoring a perfect 300 on every graded fitness test, and the third goal was to be at the top of my class in military leadership.

In all three areas, I came in at the top of my class or close to it. Writing down those goals helped make them happen. I was intent on embracing the values of West Point, and seeing those goals posted at my desk motivated me to reach them. I chose courses of action that would fulfill the vision I had put into words. In my pursuit of those multifaceted objectives of academic, physical, and leadership excellence, I was preparing for the challenges ahead. Such is the wisdom of West Point in shaping young people for the important roles they will play.

When you take the time to write down your goals, something powerful happens. They become more real to you. By putting a goal into words, you memorialize them. You feel a strong sense of commitment to reaching them. You tap into the subconscious mind, which sets to work to make them happen. Because the goals become more tangible and less abstract, you find yourself altering your behavior in ways that enhance your prospects.

> **By putting a goal into words, you memorialize them. You feel a strong sense of commitment to reaching them. You tap into the subconscious mind, which sets to work to make them happen.**

Once you have expressed your goals in writing, then revisit and review your list, updating it occasionally. Goals sometimes change.

35

What does *not* usually change is what you value, but over time, you may wish to reconsider the goals that express your values. Are you still striving for what is important to you and your family?

Write down your values, too, and weigh each goal on your list against those values. Does it still seem a worthy objective? Perhaps you already have accomplished it and it's time to identify new pursuits. Or perhaps your priorities have changed. You may need to adjust your plan of action.

At a business conference I recently attended, I met a gentleman who owns many gas stations in Southern California. Several years earlier, he told me, he jotted down the goal of reaching a net worth of $50 million. Afterward he did not consciously think about that goal, and yet he accomplished it. He recognized good business opportunities with the major oil companies, and before long, he found himself well above the goal he had set.

"It was only after it happened that I remembered what I had written," he told me. "Even though I hadn't been thinking about it, that goal was still driving me as I made those decisions." His experience, I am sure, was not unusual. When you write down goals, they tend to become self-fulfilling.

A Word of Warning

Occasionally, somebody will stumble into success, but that is rare. Most prosperous people set goals. They have a target. They begin with an objective in mind and often achieve far more. Case in point: Do you suppose Bill Gates thought that his startup, Microsoft, eventually would rank among the world's largest companies?

Once you set a goal, you very well may exceed it. The key is to be aiming at your target. If you haven't set one up, don't expect to hit the bull's-eye.

By way of warning, let me tell you about Judy, a woman in her seventies, whom I met while waiting for a flight at the Dallas airport. She was dressed well, but her eyes looked weary, not from the stress of travel but from the stress of life. "I wish I had known you a decade ago!" she told me upon learning what I did for a living. "Maybe you could have saved me from myself."

Judy proceeded to tell me the tale of her rise and fall. She once had been part of the Silicon Valley real estate scene. She acquired properties and flipped some while keeping others as rentals all over the Bay area. It was easy money, and it seemed as if the good times would never end, so she quit an excellent job with a major tech company. The properties were rising in value so fast, she figured she didn't need the income from her day job.

Unfortunately, as Judy focused on her real estate games, she never sat down to devise a bigger game plan. Instead of setting money aside and diversifying her investments, she lived a grand lifestyle, joining fancy clubs and buying expensive cars. She had millions of dollars but took no steps to plan for contingencies.

And then came 2008–2009. As the real estate market sagged, so did her fortunes. Judy was forced to sell her properties and, eventually, file for bankruptcy. No longer could she afford to live in Silicon Valley. She had to uproot and move to a rent-subsidized apartment in a small Midwestern town. Judy was not alone in her misfortune. Many others could tell a similar tale of woe. They invested poorly and too aggressively before the market crash, and a lot of them had to continue working into their late seventies to afford a meager existence.

Judy's story easily could serve as a lesson on how not to invest, but the root of her problem was not her lack of diversification. Rather, it was her utter lack of plan. She set no goals. She lacked a destination, and so she ended up in a place where she did not wish to be.

Today, at BlueSky, I regularly observe similar situations. People of retirement age come through my door, and I cannot do much to help them because of the choices they made decades ago. Now, despite their years of hard work, they have few options.

No Generic Portfolios

A lot of clients come to BlueSky after having first worked with a nonfiduciary advisor at a big bank or brokerage firm. One of the first things I ask them is, "What is your goal?" Many times, their answer is growth, aggressive growth, or income.

Those answers aren't goals. In fact, I don't know what they are. What does *aggressive* mean? Nonetheless, it happens all the time. A lot of "advisors" just want to check a box on your account application so they can pigeonhole you into one portfolio or another and move on to the next client.

That's not good enough. At BlueSky, we don't put people into generic portfolios. We work toward specific goals. You need an advisor who will spend time helping you to visualize the future. You need guidance in setting goals that include the dates you wish to accomplish them and realistic estimates of the expenses that will be involved.

Helping to identify those goals and the strategies to achieve them is the most important thing we do at BlueSky. It's the top priority. Instead of just asking when you want to retire, we go deeper with questions concerning what your reason for retiring is, what your values are, and how you envision your lifestyle after you retire. Financial planning is not merely about piling up a lot of money. I have seen time and again that people get into trouble when they cannot see beyond that. Those who do well are clear about what they will do with their money. They dream, and they plan, and they succeed.

PART TWO

. . .

GIVING IT ALL

YOU'VE GOT

By focusing first on developing yourself, you can turn your "human capital" into a wealth of financial assets. It starts with making the best choices with your money, your career, and your life.

CHAPTER 3

THE BEST INVESTMENT YOU CAN MAKE

Whatever you can do to enhance your income potential will help you to reach financial independence more quickly. To earn more, learn more. If you want your garden to grow, you must cultivate it.

For years, Tara devoted herself to her family, choosing to put her energies into raising the children while her husband provided the family income. She enjoyed playing tennis now and then at the country club. Life seemed good.

One day, her husband came home late and announced he was leaving her. Tara hadn't seen it coming. He was not wealthy, so she wouldn't get much alimony. In fact, he made only two child support payments. Tara was at a loss. What should she do? She needed to reinvent herself, but how?

During their marriage, the couple had hired a contractor to build their house. Tara had taken the reins on that project and, as a result, developed an interest in real estate. Now, with her marriage in ruins and her sense of security shaken, she set out to get her real estate license. Soon she was thriving, closing a variety of deals in the major city where she lived.

She recognized, though, that the smart money was not just in selling real estate but also in developing it. She got back in touch with the contractor who had built her house, and together they began doing some small development projects. They were making money, but Tara felt she needed to be more grounded in her understanding of the numbers, so she went back to college to get her degree in finance. With her eyes wide open to opportunities, Tara then proceeded to develop several major shopping centers, office complexes, and multiuse facilities. A visionary, she repurposed old factories into trendy office, shopping, and restaurant spaces.

Tara instinctively understood investing and the nature of risk. When she began collaborating with my firm, we helped her diversify and reduce her concentration of wealth in those buildings. She wisely built her portfolio so that her net worth was not just in real estate. This was in sharp contrast to Judy, the woman I met at the Dallas airport who had made a fortune and lost it.

Eventually, Tara sold most of her real estate holdings. She wasn't in it for the power or prestige. She used real estate as a tool to get to where she wanted to be. She was fabulously successful. In fact, for years, she was one of our firm's wealthiest clients. You would never know it. A humble and generous spirit, she reaches out to help others. She recently purchased a house for a family she knew was struggling and leased it to them for a rent that was far under market value.

Tara's real estate developments, though impressive, were not her best investment. Tara's greatest development project was Tara. Her best investment by far was in herself, and it paid huge dividends. As she learned everything she could absorb about real estate and finance, she discovered a true talent that had been dormant within her, and she capitalized on it. Out of necessity, she found a way to tap in to her innate creativity and business savvy so she could thrive in her new life.

A Bumper Crop

Tara's story illustrates a fundamental truth that governs financial success: *your earning potential is your best investment.* When you nurture your skills and talents to become your best self, your ability to earn will grow—as will your value. You are spending your money wisely when you are enhancing your ability to make money. This takes diligence and dedication. To produce a bumper crop, a garden must be carefully cultivated from one season to the next.

The money in your portfolio is your financial capital, but you are also endowed with human capital: the abilities, knowledge, and talents you can offer the world. By exercising that human capital, you convert it into economic value. Some of that money will pay for your day-to-day needs and wants, but as you develop it, you can create a surplus of value to set aside for the future. Those investments are likely to immediately begin generating an income of their own and build a substantial portfolio through the years. The more you invest in yourself, the sooner you can reach the goal of financial independence.

Here's an example of how it works. Let's say that George is a surgeon whose skills have earned him a good living. For years, however, that income was limited by how many patients he was humanly able to see and how much he was paid for each procedure. George decides to take a course on marketing and acquires a valuable new skill. As a result of his marketing efforts, he attracts many additional patients and builds a booming practice employing other surgeons. In doing so, George has multiplied his efforts, and as he generates more money, he has more to invest, further multiplying his efforts.

> **With society moving so fast, you need to continually develop new skills. Education, in whatever form, is crucial to success.**

In effect, George has not only invested in himself but has diversified himself. He has become more than a surgeon. His core competency would get him only so far. By mastering a new skill, a nonmedical one, he has enhanced his potential and strengthened his earning power. He has been able to set some of that additional income aside to grow even more.

If you want to reach maximum potential, consider yourself a worthy investment. Otherwise, you will be at risk of being left behind. With society moving so fast, you need to continually develop new skills. Education, in whatever form, is crucial to success. Financial advisory firms often talk with their clients about the costs of college, but I go further and encourage people to explore a variety of interests and educational options to broaden their perspectives and their prospects for success.

My view is this: as you get better at whatever you do, you will be ever closer to financial independence. I'm not saying you should spend money on every whim that catches your fancy. I am saying you should seize the opportunity to improve your proven abilities. This is serious business. Investing in yourself is not just a nice thing to do; it's a necessary thing to do. It's how you rise to your full potential and get that bumper crop.

Your Most Valuable Assets

As a young man in 1950, Warren Buffett was terrified of public speaking. "If I had to give a talk," he recalls, "I would throw up." He paid one hundred dollars to take a Dale Carnegie course, and it changed his life, he says. By simply learning to communicate better, he gained the confidence he needed to succeed. "I got so confident about my new ability, I proposed to my wife during the middle of the course," he said in an interview for *Forbes* magazine.[1] It also helped me sell stocks in Omaha, despite being twenty-one and looking even younger. Nobody can take away what you've got in yourself, and everybody has potential they haven't used yet." Today, Buffett's net worth has eclipsed $90 billion—not a bad ROI on a hundred bucks.

To invest in yourself, you needn't pay a bundle to acquire a college degree. Colleges have a vested interest in convincing people that a four-year degree is the only path to success. Don't buy into that. You needn't go deeply into debt to acquire new skills and knowledge. You could go to a community college or trade school, or sign up for online courses. For example, the Khan Academy offers free online education for anyone, anywhere. Explore the alternatives. Learning how to learn is a valuable skill. (We revisit the topic of college planning in Chapter 4.)

Investing in yourself can be as simple as reading a wide variety of books and journals or expanding your circle of associates. Whatever you can do to enhance your earning capacity will be an investment in

---

1   "Warren Buffett: My Greatest Investing Advice And The Investments Everyone Should Make" by Randall Lane. Sep 20, 2017. https://www.forbes.com/sites/randalllane/2017/09/20/warren-buffett-my-greatest-investing-advice-and-the-investments-everyone-should-make/#72607d40593e

yourself, and the two most valuable assets you can develop are your abilities to communicate and negotiate.

My sister Cheryl Ann has a doctorate in engineering, but much of her work depends on grant money, and it is her people skills that make all the difference in getting the funding she needs. To succeed, you need persuasive power. Those who can communicate effectively are better able to sway people to their side. Likewise, successful people tend to be good negotiators, starting with the ability to bargain for the best possible salary. Persuasion and negotiation are essential skills for advancement, and those who do them well have a definitive edge.

> **Whatever you can do to enhance your earning capacity will be an investment in yourself, and the two most valuable assets you can develop are your abilities to communicate and negotiate.**

Financial literacy is another important asset that will give you a major advantage. The fact that you are reading this book indicates you recognize the importance of understanding how money works. You want to learn not only the basics, but much more.

To make wise financial choices, you need knowledge and good advice, and it is my objective to help guide you to success in this way.

Broadening Your Horizons

In virtually any career, you must retool yourself regularly to keep up with new developments. Be alert to forces that could make your job obsolete. Look to the future and the changing labor market. For example, tobacco and textiles once were stalwarts of the North Carolina economy. Today, people in small towns are still waiting for the mills to come back. It's not going to happen. The smart ones saw what was happening and developed new skills that allowed them to keep up with the times.

Other people develop new skills not because they are *forced t*o do so, but rather because they *wish* to do so. Perhaps they have become bored or frustrated with their job and are longing for a career that is more exciting or allows them to better express who they truly are.

Such was the case with Robert, a dentist who first came to see me years ago. He was a big-hearted guy who loved life, and he was quite a character. He had back problems, so sometimes he would stretch out on the floor of my conference room as we talked about his future. Robert didn't want to be a dentist anymore. He had grown tired of sticking his fingers into people's mouths. He decided to reinvent himself by starting a distribution and warehousing company that, today, is a key link in the East Coast logistical chain. His son-in-law and daughter eventually took it over from him.

> Today, people in small towns are still waiting for the mills to come back. It's not going to happen. The smart ones saw what was happening and developed new skills.

Robert's success in the warehousing venture allowed him to pursue his passion for helping people and making his community better. He was elected to the county board of commissioners and found a way to provide laptops for every child in his rural school district. He convinced a major company to set up a new factory in his region where many people needed jobs. He also invested in real estate, including beach properties and a golf course. Robert was a dentist turned businessman, politician, and real estate investor—and he loved it. Before he passed away, we were able to help him manage his debts and also secure his assets so they would pass on efficiently to his heirs.

For most people, "investing in yourself" will not mean abandoning a career (as Robert chose to do) but augmenting it. They are not necessarily looking to change direction to get to a new destination. Rather, they are looking to advance more quickly toward the clear destination they already have in mind. By broadening their horizons, they become more rounded individuals capable of commanding a higher income. An engineer working for a major corporation, for example, might decide to study finance and thereby develop the confidence to start his own business. A finance professional who always wanted to be a farmer could use her business savvy to buy land and settle down into her dream.

> **A surefire way to lose half your net worth is to get divorced. A strong marital partnership pays dividends financially as well as emotionally.**

Successful people also invest in their relationships. They find a mentor who will encourage them to be their best and hold them accountable to making progress toward their goals. If they are married, they invest in their relationship with their spouse to keep the marriage happy and healthy. A surefire way to lose half your net worth is to get divorced. A strong marital partnership pays dividends financially as well as emotionally.

Anything that expands your mind and your range of experiences will also enhance your job performance. Go to the opera. Study a foreign language or philosophy. Take a cooking class. How will learning to bake a soufflé help you on the job? It will give your brain a workout. When you exercise any of your creative muscles, you help build your whole body of interests and initiatives. Creative activities promote success.

Investing in Your Own Business

If you have an entrepreneurial inclination, a great way to invest in yourself is to have your own business, whatever it might be. You need not start out in a big way. It could be a consulting service or other small business. The advantage of starting a small business is that you gain the ability to earn an income on your own without hitching your fortunes to someone else's success.

In today's interactive online world, it is easier than ever to launch a business. With an internet presence, you can have clients and customers all over the world. They can do business with you with a simple click on a website shopping cart. Technology has broadened the possibilities immensely so that even a small business can be on a level playing field with the big operators.

When you start your own firm, you will learn about a variety of business essentials—personnel, finance, regulations, sales, and so on—that will benefit

Technology has broadened the possibilities immensely so that even a small business can be on a level playing field with the big operators.

you greatly as you continue to grow. Even if you do not continue in the business, the skills you learn will translate into future careers and other areas of life.

My brother Mike, who is ten years younger than I am, took that route to success. After college, he worked a few years as a company accountant and then bought a Quiznos franchise. I was pleased to be able to advise him on the details of becoming a business owner. What he gained was real-life experience as an entrepreneur, but he had even bigger goals. Mike spent his nights studying to get his MBA and has become a top corporate accountant, specializing in assisting companies during mergers and acquisitions.

Entrepreneurship can pay off in many ways, and I encourage people who express an interest in starting a business to give it a shot. One of my early clients, Gordon, a former army officer—as I was— wanted to go into business for himself. To pay his bills, he sold real estate, but his dream was to launch an internet business using technology and a distribution network to generate income while he slept. He and his wife wanted to free up their time to reach out to others and share their Christian values.

Gordon began reading books on sales and marketing, but he knew he needed to know more than business essentials to succeed. So he also studied how to better relate to others. He sought out mentors to help him with the issues of business and the issues of life. His investment in himself paid off handsomely. Today, Gordon is running a highly successful company, with a real estate portfolio as well. He and his wife are realizing their dreams.

Using Our Gifts and Skills

We each have an obligation to use the gifts bestowed on us. It is our responsibility to develop the potential within us. We should be using our talents and skills to make other people's lives better. How much and how well we do that, I believe, should be the true measure of our success.

In my years, I have learned a lot about finance and business, and I also have taken to heart that big lesson on the importance of communication and negotiation. To relate well with others is essential to success. I am in the business of helping people, and to do that effectively, I must be able to hear them, understand them, reason with them, and persuade them. My insights and advice will do people no good unless I can get them to agree with me and to take action.

On my library shelves at home, many of the titles relate to relationships and self-improvement and leadership—books such as *The Magic of Thinking Big* by David Schwartz and *How to Win Friends and Influence People* by Dale Carnegie, to name just two classics in the field.

My most valuable skills are my people skills. Yes, I know a lot about investments, taxes, and estate planning, and I enjoy learning more every day. That's not all it takes, however. Early in my finance career, I was focused on the technical aspects, spreadsheets, and such; but

> **To relate well with others is essential to success. I am in the business of helping people, and to do that effectively, I must be able to hear them, understand them, reason with them, and persuade them.**

my business took off to a greater degree when I zeroed in on the power of relationships.

I have been blessed with the gift of quickly connecting with others. I can sense their feelings, and I can quickly gain their confidence in my leadership. Along the way, I have invested in myself to enhance my income potential, but I know that my responsibilities go beyond making a good living for my family. I must help others better their lives, too. My job is to take care of people as well as their portfolios.

CHAPTER 4

STAYING SMART ABOUT THE BASICS

Young people who aspire to success must know the financial fundamentals of cash flow, saving, and managing debt. The basics are critical at every stage of life. Here are some principles to govern your decisions, particularly when trying to finance your children's education while saving for retirement.

When I began working with John and Marie, they were recent college graduates in their twenties. They came to me because John's parents were longtime clients. He was thirteen years old when I started working with his mom and dad. I have a special planning program for the adult children of my clients.

John and Marie started out well. They had a combined income of about $150,000, and before marrying, they had done what many young couples neglect to do: they sought out advice while their finances were still under control and agreed to a disciplined plan that addressed long-term goals.

We began their financial journey by setting up a spending and saving plan to establish good habits. We identified ways to keep their expenses and spending in check and stay out of excessive debt. An immediate issue was Marie's student loans, which carried a relatively high interest rate. She resolved to pay them off quickly.

We set a target for their savings at 25 percent of their income, and we put that money into regular investment accounts, their workplace retirement plans, and Roth IRAs.

Before long, John and Marie welcomed their first baby into the world, and it was time to think about that child's college expenses. We discussed the advantages and disadvantages of various types of college savings plans. For flexibility, they decided to dedicate a portion of their regular savings to that goal.

Meanwhile, they were dreaming about buying their first home, so we planned for that, too. It took them about five years to save enough for the down payment, and we made sure the house was neither too expensive nor overly leveraged. It wasn't their "dream" house—not yet—but it was a fine one. I also encouraged them to buy used cars for cash to avoid having to make payments and interest.

By the time they were in their thirties, John and Marie had a reasonably priced home with a modest mortgage, no consumer or auto debt, and savings toward their children's college expenses. In addition, they already had an investment portfolio in the mid six figures. Our careful planning had put them well on their way to financial independence.

Sharpening the Saw

John and Marie started out with a big advantage over many people their age: *they knew there was much they didn't know.* That is the foundation for building true wisdom. Their story serves as an example of the importance of starting early, getting smart about the basics, and staying that way.

You may already have a good grounding in the mechanics of cash flow, income, and expenses. This chapter will offer a refresher on the fundamentals of what to do and what to advise your loved ones to do. We all need to sharpen the saw.

CASH FLOW PLANNING

The better you can manage your cash flow, the more money you will have available to convert from human capital into financial capital. In other words, by saving more of your hard-earned salary, you will build your portfolio more quickly toward the goal of financial independence.

Remember this credo: *pay yourself first.* Whether you are running a business or drawing a salary from a job, always pay yourself first. Set aside money in your 401(k) account with your employer, or in an outside investment account, or in a bank savings account. You can do it in a variety of ways. Just be sure to do it.

Set a savings target—for example, "I will save $15,000 this year"—and put it on autopilot. Some people find a recordkeeping system such as Quicken or Mint to be helpful in managing cash flow, but don't get so consumed with tracking every penny that you never look at the big picture.

For unanticipated expenses, establish a cash reserve and an emergency fund. Try to identify your short-term or one-year needs—for example, "This year I need a new roof on the house," or "This year I need to buy a car." Then anticipate your expenses for the intermediate term out to about three years and start to save for them. Then you won't be in a cash flow crunch when those costs are upon you. It's all about looking to the future and preparing.

Many people find budgeting to be difficult. In fact, they don't even like the word, which is why I call it cash flow planning and emphasize saving targets. First, consider your fixed expenses, such as mortgage, utilities, and insurance. Those costs should total no more than half of your take-home pay. You should not have a $7,000 mortgage payment, for example, if your take-home pay is $10,000 a month. Besides your fixed expenses, you also will have variable expenses: eating out, vacations, hobbies, and entertainment, to name a few. So, allocate 30 percent of your take-home pay to that category. That leaves 20 percent to devote to your financial priorities. I have found most people can work within those percentages more readily than trying to keep track of every nickel and dime.

This Easy Budgeting chart illustrates those cash-flow parameters, categorized as Essentials, Financial Priorities, and Lifestyle Choices:

EASY BUDGETING

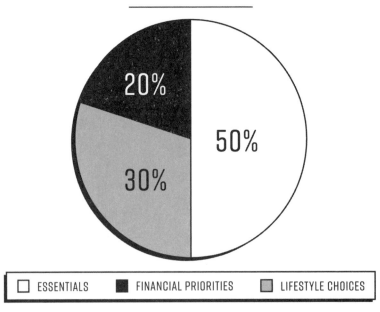

☐ ESSENTIALS	■ FINANCIAL PRIORITIES	▨ LIFESTYLE CHOICES

As you can see, no more than half of your income should go to the Essentials, which include such living expenses as your rent or mortgage, utilities, groceries, and transportation to and from your job. A maximum of 30 percent of your income should go to the flexible spending category of Lifestyle Choices, for such things as cable, internet connection, phone, childcare, entertainment, hobbies, pets, personal care, dining out, shopping, and so on. By holding to those parameters, you will have at least 20 percent of your income available to meet financial goals, including your savings, investments, and debt reduction, such as paying off a mortgage.

When Marcus and Nicole came to see me, they could not figure out where their money was going. The family had a good income, and they owned a number of investment rental properties, but they had a hard time saving. Together, we began tracking their expenses over three months to see what was going on. This was not an exercise to tell them *where* they should spend their money; rather, it helped them see where their money was already going. From there, their spending would be intentional.

Marcus and Nicole spent a lot of money on camps, lessons, and other activities for their children. They willingly sacrificed to do that. We discovered, though, that the family was spending 20 percent of their take-home pay on eating out. This was not because they enjoyed it, but because they were so disorganized at dinner time that they ordered takeout or stopped at a restaurant instead of fixing meals. They didn't want to spend their money that way. It just happened.

We found other areas to improve their cash flow. They were wasting money on insurance, for example, paying more than $30,000 a year in premiums for an array of specialty policies they did not need. They felt a strong loyalty to their insurance agent, who had been with them for years. I set up a spreadsheet to demonstrate where their coverage was overlapping.

All in all, we were able to redesign Marcus and Nicole's cash flow so they were spending money where they wanted and could free up more money to invest. That is the proven path to financial independence. When their children became adults, they became clients, too, and it was clear that they had learned powerful lessons during all those years they had observed us working together. They are highly organized in their finances, and they save and invest effectively.

MANAGING DEBT

For most people, debt is their biggest problem. Often they buy too much house and end up with an expensive mortgage payment that keeps them from accumulating true wealth. There are advantages to owning a home, and you should purchase one if that is an important goal, but beware of the debt load you will carry.

I'm not advocating you should pay cash for a house, but make sure the amount of your debt is appropriate for your income level.

Impulse buying also gets people into debt trouble. I suggest to married couples that they agree on purchases over a certain dollar amount while single people should set a personal threshold. A wise strategy is to wait until the next day before buying anything that is not on your shopping list. That helps to restrain the impulse to buy things you will have trouble paying off. We live in a one-click shopping society. It is easy to run up credit card bills, so stay away from anything that makes it easy to buy on a whim.

Similarly, many people waste money when financing automobiles. Wait until you can afford that fancy car before you spend a lot of money on it. Financially independent people do not have to finance a BMW or Mercedes. If you buy such a car before you can afford it, you are jeopardizing your long-term security. To finance that debt, you will be paying a fortune in compound interest and enriching the lender. You should be putting that principle to work in your own favor instead.

As a homeschooling dad, I've tried to explain the power of compounding. Kids tend to live in the moment and have trouble grasping a concept that involves a time frame of decades. That's hard enough for adults. Most people cannot maintain enough discipline in their saving efforts to know the true magic of compound interest. They need to experience it. It's exhilarating.

> **We live in a one-click shopping society. It is easy to run up credit card bills, so stay away from anything that makes it easy to buy on a whim.**

COLLEGE PLANNING

I worked with a couple, Don and Norma, who paid for four years of college for their son Sammy, who had declared he wanted to become a video game designer. Sammy had spent untold hours playing video games up in his bedroom and was excited about the prospect of making it his life's work to create them.

In pursuit of his youthful passion, Sammy chose an expensive arts school, and over the next four years Don and Norma spent, borrowed, or guaranteed loans up to $200,000—but Sammy couldn't find a job as a video game designer. It's a highly competitive field. After graduation, he finally got a job making about $30,000 a year.

Those college expenses compromised Don and Norma's retirement planning. We were able to arrange to get those loans paid off, and I convinced them that Sammy should be the one making the payments. The moral of this story is that although it is fine to help your kids get off to a good start, you should not put yourself in financial peril while doing so.

If your children are advancing toward college age, you may be concerned about paying for their tuition, and for good reason; it is a major expense, and you want to make sure it will be money well spent. What is your philosophy regarding college? I suggest parents discuss how they feel about this expenditure long before their kids graduate from high school. I do not recommend you simply pay the child's way wherever he or she wants to go. Set a limit on what you will spend. Do not endanger your own financial plan.

Students who invest their own earnings into their education tend to feel more motivated to succeed. When I was at Notre Dame, I saw a clear difference between the students who were struggling to pay their way, perhaps working in the cafeteria or at a job in town, and the students whose parents were just writing checks. Those who paid their own way were more appreciative of the value of their education and tended to take their studies more seriously.

Some parents tell their child they will pay for an in-state school, which likely offers a reasonable tuition rate for residents. That was the approach my own parents took with me. I was free to go out of state, but our understanding was that I would need to get scholarships to pay for any amount above the cost of an in-state school.

There are numerous strategies for saving toward college costs, including the 529 tax-advantaged plans and a variety of other educational savings accounts. You can save money in your child's name or in your own account. You can make withdrawals without penalty from your workplace retirement account if the money goes directly to educational expenses. Many parents own appreciated stock that they got from options or grants from their employer. Transferring that stock to a child for college can be a good strategy as long as you are mindful of the tax implications.

In addition, income-shifting strategies exist that allow you to employ your child if you own a business. The salary could be used for college. That's a way to get money out of your company tax free, and it can help with business planning, too.

All those methods can have tax advantages or disadvantages, so no single method is necessarily the correct way to save for college. It depends on the circumstances of the parent and child as well as the type of college. Those strategies can be bolstered with grants and scholarships.

> **I do not recommend you simply pay the child's way wherever he or she wants to go. Set a limit on what you will spend. Do not endanger your own financial plan.**

Many young people also fund college with student loans. Encourage your child to weigh the value of the degree against the amount of money he or she is borrowing. For example, the world needs good preschool teachers, but when becoming one requires a $200,000 student loan, it won't work well financially.

I never recommend that parents or anyone cosign a loan—a bad strategy all around. Instead, the student should borrow the money directly, or the parents should borrow it without the expectation that the student must pay them back. Some families draft a formal repayment plan. But beware. Borrowing and lending within the family can get emotional and stressful.

It is wise to help your children invest in themselves. A college education is one way they can get a good head start if they make the most of the experience. Or, you might encourage your child to start a business, which can be an excellent path to success as an alternative to a four-year degree. Unfortunately, many young people, even after college, lack financial literacy. As smart as they are, they likely don't know much about money, and that's an education that starts in the home.

I think back to the nuggets of wisdom my father shared as he accompanied me to the bank to invest my entrepreneurial earnings. Dad showed me by example: *Don't spend more than you make. Pay yourself first and set aside something for the future. When you can, pay in cash and be careful with debt.*

I have met a lot of highly educated people who have yet to learn those basics. These lessons for a lifetime are the building blocks for financial independence, and we need to be smart about them.

COLLEGE SAVINGS COMPARISON CHART

	529 COLLEGE SAVINGS PLAN ACCOUNT	COVERDELL EDUCATION SAVINGS ACCOUNT	UGMA/UTMA ACCOUNT	TAXABLE ACCOUNT
How can the money be used?	Can be used at almost any college or university in the US (some intl. Schools qualify as well). There are no limits.	Can be used at at almost any college or university in in the US (some intl. schools qualify as well). and can be used for K-12 educational expenses. Generally must be used before the beneficiary reaches age thirty.	The custodian must use the money for the child's benefit.	No restrictions.
How are the distributions and earnings taxed?	No federal taxes on distributions used to pay qualified education expenses. Until distribution, any earnings in your account will be tax-deferred.	No federal taxes for distributions used to pay qualified education expenses. Until distribution, any earnings will be tax-deferred.	Above a given level earnings will be taxed at either the child's or parent's rate.	Taxes apply. Earnings may be taxed as capital gains or ordinary income.
What are the contribution limits?	$400,000 per beneficiary.	$2,000 per beneficiary per year.	No limit.	No limit.
Who controls the money?	Account holder.	The authorized person controls the account.	The money belongs to the child, although it is controlled by a custodian until the child reaches the age of maturity.	Account owner.

COLLEGE SAVINGS COMPARISON CHART

	529 COLLEGE SAVINGS PLAN ACCOUNT	COVERDELL EDUCATION SAVINGS ACCOUNT	UGMA/UTMA ACCOUNT	TAXABLE ACCOUNT
Does my income level affect my ability to contribute?	No.	Your eligibility to contribute begins to phase out depending on your adjusted gross income.	No.	Account owner.
What is the impact on financial aid eligibility?	It depends on who the account holder is, but the account typically is considered a parental asset.	The account is considered the parent's asset.	The account is considered the child's asset.	The account is considered the account holder's asset.
Can I change beneficiaries?	Yes. You can transfer assets to another member of the beneficiary's family at any time.	Yes. You can transfer assets to another member of the beneficiary's family at any time.	No.	Not applicable.
What are the penalties for nonqualified withdrawals?	Federal income tax plus 10% penalty. State penalties apply.	Federal income tax plus 10% penalty.	Not applicable.	Not applicable.

CHAPTER 5

UNDERSTAND YOUR BENEFITS

Your workplace benefits can add up to a significant portion of your total compensation. Insurances, retirement plans, stock options, and many other benefits enhance the human capital you derive from your job. A word of caution: some of them may not be best for you, so choose wisely.

Floyd, a young surgeon, was excited as he reported for his first day at a major medical center, but he found it hard to focus on the flurry of forms he was asked to fill out. He was thinking about the patients he soon would be seeing. As he skimmed through the details of a huge benefits package, Floyd signed his name here and there and checked some boxes.

A year later, he came to see me, finally realizing he had made a mess of his benefits package. As I reviewed the paperwork, I quickly saw that Floyd wasn't signed up for some of the benefits he was entitled to, and he had some benefits he didn't need.

I looked at his retirement plan choices. Floyd thought he had signed up for the pretax investment plan, allowing him to save upfront on his income taxes, but he had checked the Roth after-tax box. This mistake was costing him about $20,000 a year that he could have saved in immediate tax deferrals. The Roth is a great choice for many investors, but Floyd was almost in the 50 percent marginal tax bracket and needed all the pretax deductions he could get. (We'll take a close look at retirement plan options in Chapter 11.)

I also noticed Floyd had signed up to purchase extra disability insurance beyond what his employer would cover, even though he already had a commercial plan superior to the one at the office. As a result, he had far too much coverage. He was spending money unnecessarily.

Large companies often offer a dizzying array of benefits, and people in their HR departments may be quite good, but they do not know the specifics of each employee's situation. You need someone to help you through the process. Pay close attention to the benefits as they are explained to you. Just because a company offers a benefit, it doesn't mean it is worth accepting. Most benefits will seem like great offers—free, low-cost, or tax-advantaged—but not everything is necessary or advisable.

This chapter examines a variety of those benefits. The types include health coverage, dental and vision policies, life insurance, disability insurance, 401(k) and other retirement plans, "harmless" benefits, flexible spending accounts, and equity compensation.

TYPICAL WORKPLACE BENEFITS
Health insurance
Dental and vision policies
Life insurance
Disability insurance
401(k) and other retirement plans
No-cost employee benefits
Flexible spending accounts
Equity compensation

Health Insurance

With the cost of health care rising precipitously, health insurance benefits are certainly a welcome addition. In many states, employers are mandated to subsidize at least half of the employee's cost, and many employers will cover the full cost. The insurance choices are many, and we will touch base on those in Chapter 12. What is right for you will depend on your health situation, how much you use health care, and which network includes the doctors and facilities you prefer.

Generally, health benefits are a great deal for employees. If your spouse also has coverage under an employee plan, take time to compare the terms to see which is best for your family. I have seen situations where both spouses get coverage from the same employer, and others where it's more beneficial for each to take their own employer-provided coverage.

Dental and Vision Policies

If dental and vision policies are cheap and heavily subsidized, they are fine to accept, but as a rule, such coverage is limited. Policies that are not subsidized by your employer are not usually a great deal.

If you sign up for dental and vision coverage, be sure you need it and will be using it. I see a lot of clients who are paying for a plan but only need preventive care, which can be cheaper by simply paying out of pocket.

Life Insurance

Your company may provide a certain amount of life insurance benefits to you automatically, typically a multiple of your salary. This is likely group life insurance, and it's usually at a fairly low cost, so I recommend you take that.

Insurance companies make money by getting you to sign up for extra policies for your spouse and children, as we will see in Chapter 12. Sometimes those add-ons are not the best available to you. Be sure to compare the costs and coverage to what you could get from a policy not covered by your employer.

Often, employers will offer accidental death and dismemberment insurance. If it is free, take it, but if you have to sign up and pay for it, I recommend you do not. Such policies usually cost a lot for what you get in benefits. They play on people's fear of accidents, and the insurer will pay nothing, of course, if you die of natural causes or disease.

Frankly, what you need more is life insurance. If you're dead, you're dead, and it doesn't matter how you died.

Disability Insurance

Most employers will pay for disability insurance, and it's usually a decent benefit. It tends to cost a lot if you get it on your own. Remember, however, that compensation from a disability insurance plan paid with pretax dollars is considered taxable income.

One of my clients, Samir, was a doctor in a private practice that offered a modest disability policy to cover some of his salary. He could increase that coverage for a price, but after examining the terms, I recommended he get his own policy, which offered more for less money. He agreed, paying the premium with after-tax dollars.

A year or two later, this brilliant physician, in the prime of his life and career, was diagnosed with cancer and lymphoma. He needed that supplemental policy. It paid him $20,000 (tax-free) a month on top of the $10,000 a month paid from a taxable benefit that his work policy provided.

Samir remained optimistic he would return to work someday. He would even sit up in his hospital bed with his tablet to participate in conferences with his partners. It was not to happen. About a year after his cancer diagnosis, he died. He and his wife had two kids in college. As his loved ones mourned, at least they knew that Samir had planned well. My firm assisted his widow in selling the practice, which was owned by several partners, and the subsequent winding up of the company's affairs.

There is no reason, of course, not to accept the disability benefits paid by your employer. However, you may need more coverage. If you do, shop around. Check out all your options. Some states, such as California, automatically provide for short-term disability benefits, so check to see if your state has such a program and whether it will cover your needs.

401(k) and Other Retirement Plans

Most employers offer some sort of retirement plan, such as the 401(k), 403(b), 457, money purchase pension plan, or profit sharing plan. Don't miss out on such workplace programs, particularly if your employer offers a matching contribution. That is basically free money.

A few generations ago, workers based their retirement planning on the company pension. Today, most companies have done away with those "defined-benefit" plans. They have replaced them with "defined contribution" plans, so-called because the employees regularly devote a percentage of their paychecks to a menu of investment options. Whereas companies used to provide the retirement benefit, now it is generally up to the employees to make the investment decisions. In Chapter 7, we will look at how to choose investments wisely.

The 401(k) is the most common of these plans. It is called a tax-advantaged plan because the employees get an immediate deduction for the amount of the contributions in the year they are made, and they pay no further tax until they withdraw from the account during retirement. As of 2018, most plans allow employees under the age of fifty to put in $18,500 a year, or $24,500 for those who are fifty or older, not including employer matches. A special program for governmental and nonprofit employees (the 457 and 403(b) plans) allows them to defer as much as $37,000 a year, as of 2018, if they are under fifty, or $61,500 if they are fifty or over, using the special three-year catch-up rule. And that doesn't even include any matching contributions from the employer.

Be aware that the brokerages and life insurance companies offering the menu choices have extracted a lot of fees from participants in such plans through the years. Not all plans are equal. There are bad ones, particularly some offered by nonprofits and governmental organizations (with the exception of the federal government). In Chapter 13, we will look at some of the forces that can derail your plans.

Many of the employer-sponsored plans offer both pretax and post-tax options. With the pretax option, you get a deduction now and pay no tax until you pull out your money in retirement. With the post-tax (Roth) option, you don't get that immediate deduction. However, you pay no tax on the money or on its growth when you withdraw it.

If you had a crystal ball, it would be easy to decide which tax option to take. If you knew you would be in a lower tax bracket during retirement, you would choose the pretax option and get your deduction now. If you knew you would be in a higher bracket, you would choose the post-tax option and pay your obligation now to avoid it in the future. Nobody can be sure what the future holds, but you can make an educated guess based on current conditions.

For example, in the 2018 tax environment, we would usually recommend the pretax option to get the instant deduction if you are in the 24 percent federal bracket or higher. Your state tax bracket also must be figured into the equation. The higher the state income tax bracket, the more the scale tips toward the pretax option, especially if you plan to retire to a state with a lower tax rate.

	SIMPLE-IRA	SEP-IRA	SOLO 401(K)	401(K) PLAN	SAFE HARBOR 401(K) PLAN	PROFIT SHARING PLAN	CASH BALANCE PLAN
Target or Typical Plan Sponsor	All businesses with fewer than 100 employees.	All businesses.	All businesses with no common law employees.	All businesses, except governmental agencies.	All businesses, except governmental agencies.	All businesses.	All highly profitable businesses with consistent profit patterns.
Advantages	Provides pre-tax retirement savings and easy administration. No tax filings required.	Allows sole- proprietors the ability to contribute max. deferrals plus 20% to 25% of their income to a bankruptcy proof trust. No tax filings until assets reach $250,000.	Varies depending on situation.	Provides an effective tax tool and employee benefit with employer control. Roth contributions allowed for high income taxpayers.	Great for small, family owned businesses who wish to avoid ADP/ACP and Top-Heavy discrimination tests. Roth contributions allowed.	Often added to a 401(k) giving the sponsor the discretion to contribute a total of 25% of eligible plan compensation. Contribution amounts can vary greatly among owners and eligible employees.	Allows owners who are over forty to contribute much higher contributions per year.
Funded by	Employee and employer.	Employee.	Employee and employer.	Employee and employer.	Employee and employer.	Employer.	Employer.
Eligibility Requirements	Employees earning $5,000 in two prior years.	May impose age twenty-one with any service in three out of five years.		May impose age twenty-one and one year of service with 1,000 hours.	May impose age twenty-one and one year of service with 1,000 hours.	May impose age twenty-one and one year of service with 1,000 hours. Two years is 100% vesting.	May impose age twenty-one and one year of service with 1,000 hours.
Maximum Annual Individual Contribution	100% of compensation up to $12,500 (indexed). Additional $3,000 in catch-up deferrals if age over fifty.	Not applicable.	100% of income up to $18,500 in employee deferrals (indexed). Additional $6,000 in catch-up deferrals if age over fifty.	100% of compensation up to $18,500 in employee deferrals (indexed). Additional $6,000 in catch-up deferrals if age over fifty.	100% of compensation up to $18,500 in employee deferrals (indexed). Additional $6,000 in catch-up deferrals if age over fifty.	Not applicable.	Not applicable.

All figures are current as of 2018

Maximum Annual Employer Contribution	Choice of two required contributions: match 100% up to 3% of compensation or contribution of 2% of compensation to all eligible employees. If the 3% option is chosen, the match can be reduced in two out of five years but no lower than 1%.	Discretionary employer contributions up to 25% of eligible employee compensation.	20% of Schedule C income or K-1 income and 25% of W-2 income plus $18,500 in employee deferrals (indexed). Additional $6,000 in catch-up deferrals if age fifty at any time during the year. Income is limited to $275,000 (indexed).	25% of eligible employee condensation. Individual eligible employee condensation is limited to $270K (indexed). Individual total contributions may not exceed $55,000 /$61,000 eligible (indexed).	Choice of one Safe Harbor Match formular or SH Non-Elective: 1(a). Basic Match 100% up to 3% of compensation plus 50% of next 2% of compensation. 1(b). Enhanced Match 100% up to 4% of compensation (the enhanced match is easier to explain and setup on payroll). 2. Contribution of 3% of compensation to all eligible employees.	Not applicable.
Vesting Schedule & Conditions	100% immediate vesting.	100% immediate vesting.	100% immediate vesting.	Vesting schedule available. Employer contributions may be subject to requirements such as 1,000 hours of service and/or employment on the last day of the plan year.	100% immediate vesting on all Safe Harbor contributions. Additional discretionary employer contributions may be subject to a vesting schedule.	Vesting schedule available. Contributions may be subject to requirements such as 1,000 hours of service and/or employment on the last day of the plan year.
Discrimination Testing & Government Reporting	ADP: No Top Heavy: No Govt. Reporting: No	ADP/ACP: No Top Heavy: Yes Govt. Reporting: No	ADP/ACP: No Top Heavy: No Govt. Reporting: If >250K	ADP/ACP: Yes Top Heavy: Yes Govt. Reporting: Yes	ADP/ACP: No Top Heavy: No Govt. Reporting: Yes	ADP/ACP: No Top Heavy: Yes Govt. Reporting: Yes
Loans Available	No	No	Yes	Yes	Yes	Yes
When to Establish	No later than October 1st.	Any time prior to tax filing.	Prior to fiscal year end.	Prior to fiscal year end.	No later than 3 months prior to plan year end	Prior to fiscal year end.

Additional rightmost columns:

	Vesting Schedule & Conditions	Discrimination Testing & Government Reporting	Loans Available	When to Establish
Not applicable.	Vesting schedule available. Employer contributions are not subject to requirements in most cases in order to pass the discrimination test.	ADP/ACP: No Top Heavy: No Govt. Reporting: Yes	Yes	Prior to fiscal year end.

All figures are current as of 2018

To make the right decisions regarding your workplace retirement plan, it's best to conduct detailed planning that looks at long-term strategies. Generally, however, these plans are a huge benefit, and you should take advantage of the opportunity to set money aside and invest for your future.

No-Cost Employee Benefits

No-cost employee benefits include wellness programs, discounts, and freebies. Perhaps your office complex has a fitness center, and you can use it without charge. Maybe you work for an airline and can fly free on standby. These are no-cost or discount programs, and most of them are not taxable. Take advantage of them as much as possible.

Flexible Spending Accounts

Your employer may offer you one of a few types of flexible spending accounts (FSAs) or cafeteria plans. A cafeteria plan is simply a written plan that allows employees to choose between receiving taxable compensation or a qualified benefit they can exclude from their wages.

The two most popular are medical FSAs and dependent day care FSAs. In both plans, the employee can designate a dollar amount to contribute annually. For example, let's say you estimate you will have $2,000 in out-of-pocket medical expenses in the coming year. You can have your employer put that amount into your tax-free FSA instead of including it in your paycheck. Then, during the year, you cover your out-of-pocket medical costs from what you set aside in the FSA. Similarly, if you have day care expenses, you can divert some of your salary into an FSA to cover them.

Although FSAs are a good deal, be careful not to overfund them. They have a "use it or lose it" stipulation. A lot of plans do offer a partial carryover from year to year, but nonetheless, be as accurate as possible in estimating how much money you will need or risk losing it.

Equity Compensation

Equity compensation is common in publicly traded companies. A lot of startup, technology, and private companies likewise offer this benefit, although for them it is a more complicated arrangement.

Here, we look at how the benefit works with some of the larger, well-known plans available at public companies such as Google, Apple, and Amazon. In essence, the company may offer compensation in some form of company stock, and this can be done in a variety of ways.

STOCK OPTIONS

The first category is called stock options, which are less common than they used to be. That's because of accounting rule changes that make them less favorable from the corporate tax standpoint. There are two basic types: nonqualified stock options and incentive stock options.

With a nonqualified stock option, the company gives you the right, but does not obligate you, to buy a specific number of its shares for a particular price within a certain time frame. For example, the company may offer an employee the right to buy 1,000 shares for $5 a share for the next five years. The stock may be worth $25 or $50 a share, so the employee is getting an opportunity to buy it cheaper than it would cost on the open market. The risk is that the value could decline to the point where the option would be worthless.

Taxation of stock options is complicated, but suffice it to say that on nonqualified options, the employees report ordinary income as the fair market value of the stock minus what they paid. If the stock was worth $50 a share, for example, an employee with a $5 option would pay income tax on $45 a share. To cover the tax bill, it can make sense to exercise the options and sell a certain amount of the stock immediately.

Incentive stock options are less popular, but they offer favorable tax treatment. If you hold the stock you acquired by exercising your incentive stock options beyond the later of (1) one year from the date they're exercised or (2) two years from the grant date (when they were granted to you but could not be exercised until vest date), you pay capital gains tax instead of ordinary income tax. As of 2018, the capital gains rate is lower than for ordinary income, so incentive stock options can be beneficial that way. Ask your advisor for a full explanation.

Stock options can present pitfalls associated with the alternative minimum tax (AMT) and some good opportunities with an 83(b) election. These are too technical to cover here, so be sure to get professional help if you are awarded stock options.

With both categories, we recommend taking the money off the table, as explained in Chapter 6. Having a lot of your money tied up in company stock is unlikely to be a good idea, so exercise these options as you can, moving away from the company stock into a more diversified portfolio. The next chapter looks at the story of Enron and what happened to its employees who were holding too much of their employer's stock.

EMPLOYEE STOCK PURCHASE PLAN (ESPP)

The employee stock purchase plan (ESPP) is more common today than nonqualified or incentive stock options.

The ESPP falls into the same category as a stock option but is simpler. If your company offers this type of plan, you can buy stock through payroll deductions at a discount of usually 10 to 15 percent of the current trading price. The purchase is based on a predetermined schedule. That means if you enroll in the plan, it will automatically purchase a set dollar amount of shares, typically every six months.

I usually recommend selling the shares soon after purchase and redirecting the proceeds to your diversified portfolio. This has tax consequences, however. With an ESPP, when you sell your shares, the discount you received from the market price when you bought the shares is taxed as ordinary income. Any additional gain is taxed as short- or long-term capital gain depending on your holding period.

If you sell immediately, as I recommend, you may incur a nominal amount of short-term capital gains tax. If you wait a year from the date of purchase and two years from the grant date (when they were granted to you), you can get long-term capital gain treatment, which is lower than short-term. Nonetheless, there is often a greater advantage in selling right away and diversifying.

RESTRICTED STOCK UNITS (RSU)

The last category of equity compensation is called restricted stock units (RSUs), and these are also more common than nonqualified or incentive stock options. Google uses them, calling them Google stock units (GSUs).

83

TYPE OF GRANT	GRANT	VESTING	TAX TREATMENT EXERCISE/PURCHASE	WITHHOLDING	SALE
Restricted Stock Units	No	OI, FICA	N/A	At vesting	CG
Restricted Stock Units without section 83(b) election	No	OI, FICA	N/A	At vesting	CG
Restricted Stock Units with section 83(b) election	OI, FICA	No	N/A	At grant	CG
Performance Shares	No	OI, FICA	N/A	At payout	CG
Performance Share Units	No	OI, FICA	N/A	At payout	CG
Incentive Stock Options	No	No	None,* AMT (possibly), or OI	No	Possibly CG, AMT and/or OI
Nonqualified Stock Options	No	No	OI, FICA	At exercise	CG
Stock Appreciation Rights	No	No	OI, FICA	At exercise	CG
Tax-Qualified ESPP	No	N/A	None or OI*	No	CG
Nonqualified ESPP	No	N/A	OI, FICA	At purchase	CG

OI = Ordinary Income Tax   CG = Capital Gains Tax or Capital Loss Reporting (report on Form 8949 and schedule D of tax return)
AMT = Alternative Minimum Tax   FICA = Social Security up to yearly maximum, plus Medicare

Special holding periods apply. Tax treatment depends on when shares are sold and on the price at sale relative to the price at exercise/purchase. Assumes shares are delivered at vesting and not further deferred (under a Nonqualified Deferred Compensation plan). With proper deferral, OI is delayed until later.

RSUs are awards of stock that have a vesting schedule. When the restricted stock is granted, you can't do what you want with it immediately. A vesting schedule is the timeframe over which the shares become fully yours.

For example, if you are granted one hundred shares of stock, a four-year vesting schedule will free up 25 percent of the shares for each of the next four years that you stay employed. If you leave the company, you lose the shares. These are used as an incentive to keep you from leaving the company. When those shares vest, you are liable for ordinary income tax on the value of those shares.

Generally, a certain number of shares are sold automatically on the vest date to cover the taxes. You're left with a percentage of the original amount granted, which you can sell immediately or retain for future growth. As we did for the ESPP plan described above, we recommend selling them at the time it vests and transferring the funds into a more diversified portfolio.

Vigilance at Every Step

Always keep in mind that your employee benefits, in the many forms they can take, are part of your overall compensation. They can be as simple as a flexible vacation plan or as complicated as the various types of equity plans. In some cases, corporate benefits can add a value of 50 percent or more on top of your salary. On average, they will add 10 to 15 percent.

For business owners, the rules vary. Owner-employees are excluded from participating in some benefit packages, depending on the corporate structure. A regular C corporation is the friendliest to owner-employees. In addition, if you operate a business, you will be subject to complicated discrimination rules that go beyond the scope of this book but which you should understand.

Despite the significant value you stand to gain from your benefits, be vigilant. Make sure, for example, that a vendor hasn't made its way into your company selling an inferior insurance policy or a fee-heavy 401(k). Understand the tax consequences of your retirement plan and any equity compensation you receive.

It is important to take the time to understand the range of your company's benefits. Proceed wisely and seek good advice at every step.

PART THREE

...

PUTTING YOUR
MONEY TO WORK

Once you know where you're going in life and are pursuing your full potential, it is time to develop your financial capital. A wise investment strategy can bring you significant income outside your job or business. You work hard for your money. Be sure it works hard for you.

CHAPTER 6

THE VALUE OF A SENSIBLE STRATEGY

Before investing a cent, you need a strategy. To simply chase returns is folly. Successful investors put the purpose first. You must develop a plan for how and when you will use the money, how much return you need to meet your objectives, and the amount of risk that you—and your portfolio—can withstand.

The sleet stung our faces as we wandered all night through the mountains of Dahlonega, Georgia. Taking turns leading the patrol, we splashed through icy streams and crisscrossed the ridges, but none of us was privy to where we were going.

We did know this: anyone who so much as whispered "I quit" would vanish.

US Army Ranger School pushed us to our physical and mental limits. Most of the young soldiers didn't make it through the training, and we saw many men reach the breaking point. Some would sit and refuse to move, a reaction that, if it were to happen in combat, would put their comrades at risk. We would hear the chopper coming to take those men away, or sometimes they departed in an army truck that lumbered up the mountainside at night. "Get in the truck!" someone would shout, and we would hear the tailgate dropping. I know my buddies were thinking what I was thinking: *man, those guys are going to be warm and eating a meal in about twenty minutes.*

Our human capacities are far greater than we might imagine. That was the lesson we learned. In our daily lives, we use but a fraction of our physical and mental abilities. The US Army Ranger training had a crucial purpose: we had to be ready for whatever came our way. We experienced what it was like to try to function when we were utterly exhausted, famished, cold, and lost, and so we resolved to do our utmost to be alert and prepared at all times. In a war zone, we would know how to handle stress because we had experienced it before.

The irony is that much of military duty is routine and far from exciting. It entails long stretches of boredom punctuated by intensely stressful periods and moments of sheer terror. The adventures are exciting but not continuous.

We were never just sitting around doing nothing, though. We continually trained. We drilled. We rehearsed to the point that when the real deal did present itself, we could react virtually by reflex— swiftly and decisively. We knew exactly what to do and were ready to fulfill the mission. We had a strategy.

I am forever grateful to have had that opportunity to serve my country. Many other dedicated soldiers have since stepped in line to take on that immense responsibility. Although I have moved on, I will never forget the lesson that is central to so much in life: *be prepared, have a plan, and follow a strategy.* We inhabit a world of great opportunity but also one of dire risk, and we must face it boldly, not blindly.

Much of financial planning is less than exciting. Yes, it can be downright boring. And yes, you must do it because that is how you get ready for whatever life might send your way. For years, you have worked hard for your money, on the job or in your business. Now you need to follow the drill to make sure that your money works hard for you. It's time to prepare so that you know exactly what to do.

Lessons from the Past

Never forget: a bad decision can wreck you financially.

Many people still shiver recalling the fate of the energy company Enron, which in the late 1990s and early 2000s, was the rage among investors. It would become a household name—but for the wrong reasons. Enron became the poster child of what *not* to do.

For years, Enron was the darling of Wall Street. As its stock kept rising, its employees put much of their retirement savings into it.

> **Much of financial planning is less than exciting. Yes, it can be downright boring. And yes, you must do it because that is how you get ready for whatever life might send your way.**

They were buying Enron stock in their 401(k)s with their own salary deferral money, and Enron's matching contributions were made in stock rather than cash. Neither practice by employees or employer is illegal, but it's definitely not smart, because it concentrated employees' retirement savings too much in the stock of the company they worked for. That lack of diversification was a nightmare in the making. Another problem: Enron wouldn't let the employees sell the stock until they reached the age of fifty.

As a result, the employees' retirement accounts became increasingly concentrated in company shares. In 2001, 62 percent of the 401(k) plan assets were in Enron stock. Chasing the promises of riches, people were betting too heavily on the company.

Then, due to fraudulent bookkeeping, Enron stock began to collapse. The employees were not just facing unemployment; they were facing financial ruin. Many had all their money invested in the stock. And yet, even on the way down, Enron shares still were touted as a great investment that would be rising again at some point. As late as September 2001, a few months before the company filed for bankruptcy, the CEO was still promoting the stock to the employees— and they were still buying it.

By the time of the bankruptcy filing, Enron stock was virtually worthless, trading for less than a dollar, down from its peak of over ninety dollars a share in mid-2000. So much can change in a year. Many employees lost not only their jobs but also most of their retirement savings.

Enron was one of the largest bankruptcies in US history. Other notables include WorldCom the following year and General Motors in 2009. Airlines have gone bankrupt, too. But the example of Enron most powerfully illustrates the theme of this chapter: you must have a plan to insulate yourself against disasters.

Learning from Enron

What should investors have learned from the Enron example? For one, you cannot count on Wall Street to be your friend. Remember, Wall Street investors continued to promote Enron even as it was collapsing. Also avoid concentrating your assets in a single investment. Enron did not endorse a diversification plan. I warn my clients not to invest in any single stock, and I recommend they put their money in more than the stock market. In today's world, the "heroes" of Wall Street can end up in bankruptcy seemingly overnight.

I am not singling out the Enron employees for blame because they took a high-risk path with their investments. They were misled, and criminal activity at the company contributed. Nonetheless, the employees were not merely victims, either. Most of them had no plan for their investments; they were blindly sinking their money into Enron shares. *For lack of a strategy, they sacrificed their dreams.*

Never forget this Enron lesson: diversification is essential for your protection. It promotes strong performance, as well. No evidence exists that anyone, over long periods, has been able to consistently outperform a broadly diversified investment strategy.

A world of investments is open today to professional and amateur investors alike. With the click of a mouse, investors can choose domestically and globally among a wide variety of companies. They can include asset classes such as emerging markets, smaller companies, and bonds with the potential to provide stability to a portfolio. Investment providers such as the Vanguard Group and Charles Schwab & Co. offer mutual funds and exchange traded funds that are virtually free of fees.

> **A world of investments is open today to professional and amateur investors alike. With the click of a mouse, investors can choose domestically and globally among a wide variety of companies.**

Do not be misled. Among those many opportunities lurk many risks. That is why you need a solid investment plan with a diversified portfolio to offset them. You require a sensible strategy for your investments so you can pursue the good life while dealing with all the dangers along the way.

When you temper your confidence with prudence, you won't wake up one day to discover, short of a global economic collapse, that you are broke.

Your Investment Policy Statement

An important step in designing a coherent plan is to devise an investment policy statement (IPS). Your IPS will address five essential elements that wise investors consider before buying: (1) the purpose of the investment, (2) how long the money will be invested, (3) the rate of return needed to achieve your goal, (4) your risk tolerance, and (5) your risk capacity.

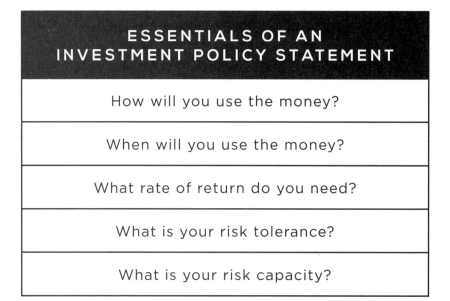

ESSENTIALS OF AN INVESTMENT POLICY STATEMENT
How will you use the money?
When will you use the money?
What rate of return do you need?
What is your risk tolerance?
What is your risk capacity?

For every investment, first determine what you want to accomplish with that money. How do you intend to use it? To buy a house next year? To send your kids to college? To fund your retirement needs? Different money can have different objectives. Simultaneously, you might be saving for all those goals and more.

Some of the money in your portfolio will be needed soon and some perhaps not for decades. For each purpose, you need to figure *when* you will need the money. If you need it soon, it should be in a liquid, accessible account.

Next, to meet each objective, how much must your money grow? The necessary rate of return will depend on how much you are investing, how much you will need, and how soon. Let's say you have saved $100,000 and that's all you need for your down payment on the house next year. That means you require a return of 0 percent, so don't take unnecessary risks with that money. If you have saved all you can but know you will require $110,000, then you will need an annual return, after expenses, of 10 percent. Yet it would come at a level of risk that could scuttle your dream. (To figure your return, online calculators can be helpful, but consult with an advisor in complicated situations.)

How much risk can you tolerate? Risk has two components, and one of them is your risk tolerance. If your million-dollar portfolio were to begin sinking to $900,000 to $800,000 to $700,000, how much willpower would you have to stick with your strategy? That is an important question. You can get into big trouble by changing your strategy based on an emotional response.

The other component is your risk capacity. You might have plenty of risk tolerance and have resolved to keep all your money in stocks for the long term. And you also might have triplets who are getting ready to go to college next year. Maybe you are working for a Silicon Valley startup that could go out of business any day, and your mother has dementia and will be moving into your house next month. As you can see, your capacity to take on risk is low. Yes, you might be able to tolerate it, but your portfolio cannot. If things were to go wrong with your investments, you couldn't cover all your short-term expenses.

Active Versus Passive Investing

At this point, let me debunk a myth that has prevented countless portfolios from rising to their potential. This is the myth that "active" investment, not "passive" investment, is the pathway to riches. Active investment is the world of professional pickers and prognosticators who try to beat the markets. Passive investment is essentially accepting the markets and their power to prevail over time. It means investing in passively managed (index) funds that are designed to track the broad performance of a basket of predefined securities.

Most people believe they succeed at investing by keeping an eagle eye on the performance of individual securities and making great decisions on which to buy and which to sell and when. That seems to make sense, right? How could anyone argue against vigilance and stepping forward to make committed choices? *Active* investing sounds so energizing, so decisive. Who wants to be *passive?*

You do.

Investment consultant Charles Ellis, author of *Winning the Loser's Game*, points out that professional tennis players win by aces, rushing the net, and smashing the ball. Amateurs, however, win by making the fewest errors. Investing is like that. To win, you don't want to compete with the professionals. The way to win at investing is to develop a broadly diversified strategy. You succeed by having a plan, sticking to it, and avoiding errors. You invest passively, favoring the index funds and tapping into the prevailing power of the market rather than trying to outwit it.

Every day, a lot of extremely smart people with MBAs and PhDs go to work at institutional investment companies, trading financial instruments using sophisticated computer algorithms. Half a trillion dollars moves daily in the securities markets. With that many people doing that much trading, the going price for a security is highly likely to be fair and properly

> **Active investing sounds so energizing, so decisive. Who wants to be passive? You do.**

based on all that is currently known about it. That is the principle of the "efficient market": when you buy a share of a company, the price (more often than not) will reflect all relevant information about the current and future prospects for the enterprise.

What does that mean? Don't try to outguess the market. Even the professionals can't do it. On average, over a fifteen-year time horizon, only 15 percent or so of equity mutual funds have outperformed, or even kept pace with, the market average. Most go out of business or merge into another fund. Few do better than the market itself. Those that appear to outperform the market once are unlikely to do so again, so the fact that a fund has outperformed in the past is not an indication of what will happen in the future.

Stars rise, and stars fall. The well-known investor Bill Miller, who operated the Legg Mason Value Trust Fund, beat the S&P 500 index for fifteen straight years, from 1991 to 2005. For such a feat, he was praised, for a time, as the greatest manager ever. But Miller did not do well in the ensuing years. In fact, in the two or three years of the economic downturn, he lost so much money that he wiped out that fifteen-year track record.

The lesson again is clear: don't chase investment performance. Fund managers have not shown that they can consistently and reliably outperform the markets as a whole. Instead, let the markets work for you. Over long periods, stocks and bonds and different types of financial assets have provided a positive return—not every year, or every month, or every day, but over time. The market itself, over the years, can do what the latest hot manager cannot.

At BlueSky, we use the chart (on the opposite page) to explain the basics of "active" versus "passive" investing. To be a successful investor, stay in Quadrant 4. Don't try to pick stocks or time the markets.

Cool Investors Prevail

So many investors jump on the bandwagon or jump ship. They base their actions on headlines and the pronouncements of the talking heads: "These are the top ten funds!" or "Buy gold today!" or "Sell now before the collapse!" But it is a fool's errand to try to predict the direction of markets; there are too many variables at play. The gurus and pundits will make the same predictions year after year, and of course, they will be right at some point and expound upon how wise they were. Remember, even a broken clock is right twice a day.

> **The market itself, over the years, can do what the latest hot manager cannot.**

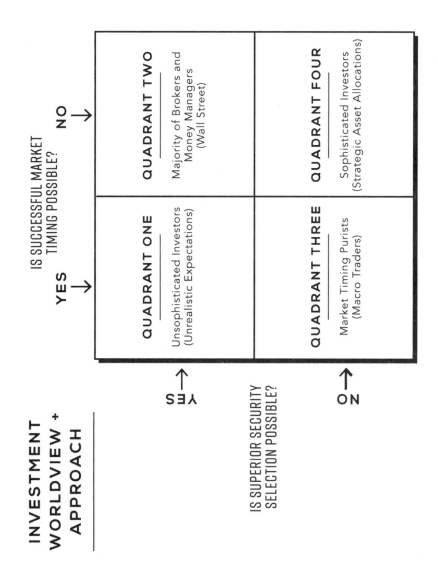

INVESTMENT
WORLDVIEW +
APPROACH

IS SUCCESSFUL MARKET
TIMING POSSIBLE?

YES →   NO →

QUADRANT ONE

Unsophisticated Investors
(Unrealistic Expectations)

QUADRANT TWO

Majority of Brokers and
Money Managers
(Wall Street)

QUADRANT THREE

Market Timing Purists
(Macro Traders)

QUADRANT FOUR

Sophisticated Investors
(Strategic Asset Allocations)

IS SUPERIOR SECURITY
SELECTION POSSIBLE?

↑ YES

↑ NO

CYCLE OF INVESTOR PSYCHOLOGY

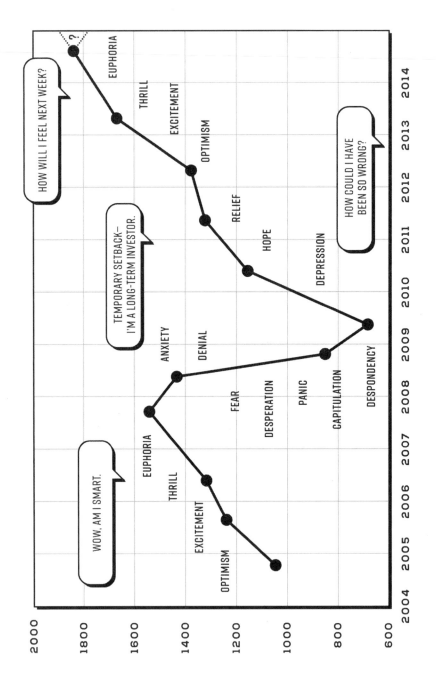

The way you invest most of your money should be relatively boring. Don't let your emotions get in the way! As prices edge up, investors feel optimistic. They rush to buy, pushing prices even higher. The economy is booming, and they feel elated. Then prices slip. They feel nervous and sell while they can, and prices fall more. As fear breeds panic, the markets slump. And the cycle repeats itself.

That is a typical pattern that has much to do with driving the economy. Emotions lead investors to buy at the peak and sell in the trough, and thus are fortunes lost.

Think of investing as a way to grow your savings, not a way to make money. A lot of people try to make their portfolio do something it's not designed to do. For example, if you save $1,000 and expect that to turn into $100,000 by finding just the right investment, you're kidding yourself. You are asking your portfolio to perform a miracle. Have realistic expectations for the return on your investment.

It's No Bag of Tricks

The investing world has been changing for decades. Once, people traded less. They bought shares in several big companies they deemed to be reliable, put the certificates in a safety deposit box, and held onto the stock for many years.

Today, many of the Wall Street financial players seem uninterested in the fortunes of the individual companies or the families whose money is at stake. They are intent on outdoing one another and making money, and investors often gallop right along with them.

Always remember that it is folly to chase after the next hot investment or the new hot manager. You are unlikely to do well with most of the hedge funds and macro traders who are looking to time the market. Neither you nor your guru nor Wall Street's brightest can outsmart and outperform the market consistently and reliably.

Investing in the equity of companies is a worthwhile undertaking, but you must proceed with caution. Your investments need to be part of a greater plan that includes your strategy for life and begins with realistic expectations for your portfolio. I embrace strategic asset allocation, which sets reasonable objectives for returns in various investment classes and regularly rebalances the portfolio to maintain those targets. It is an approach espoused by Warren Buffett, Jack Bogle of Vanguard, and other leading thinkers such as Eugene Fama, Kenneth French, and Charles Ellis. (We will take a close look at designing your portfolio in Chapter 7.)

If you are reading this book, you probably are a high achiever, so consider this: those who achieve an average return are doing better than 90 percent of the investors out there. The investors who come out ahead are not the ones in search of management magic. The true achievers tend to be those who accept the market for what it is.

The investment arena does indeed offer huge opportunities, but it is not a bag of get-rich-quick tricks. Success comes from setting goals and faithfully following a plan.

The investment arena does indeed offer huge opportunities, but it is not a bag of get-rich-quick tricks. Success comes from setting goals and faithfully following a plan that prevents you from making mistakes. Success comes from controlling your emotions, deciding how much risk you and your portfolio can withstand, and resisting temptations to take any more of it than necessary.

Success comes, too, from controlling your expectations so you are not on a quest for the impossible dream.

When you have a plan, you emerge from the dark of the great unknown. You cannot know everything that may come your way, but you will know the drill and be able to proceed with confidence. Having a strategy combats stress, even in challenging times, whether it's in the depth of a recession or on a mountaintop during a sleet storm. Such is the power of preparedness. Come what may, you are ready.

CHAPTER 7

SELECTING INVESTMENTS WISELY

Once you have developed a plan for your investments and know where you want them to take you, get down to the details of designing your portfolio and your mix of stocks and bonds. In doing so, don't guess what might be best for you. You should know.

"It's all going to collapse," my friend Carl warned me one day. "What?"

"The global financial system. What are you doing about it?"

I took a deep breath. He was a good guy and well connected in Washington, DC, but even during the throes of the financial crisis of 2009, this was a bit much.

"I don't have a crystal ball, Carl."

"You don't need one!" he said. "I've got this straight from congressmen and senators, and they've got the inside dope on this. It's happening, man. What are you doing for your clients?"

"Look, Carl ... sure, a lot of people are in pain out there. But who's to say? I mean, right now there's no convincing evidence either way whether it would be better to get out of the markets or get into them."

That's not what I'm hearing," he said. "I'm selling everything. I'm cashing out all my investments. Just thought I'd ask if that's what you're telling folks, too."

I wasn't.

I'm a believer in "evidence-based" investing. It's a term borrowed from the medical field where decisions are based not on hunches or speculation, but on evidence from research and clinical trials. Likewise, in evidence-based investing, decisions are based on well-documented research. And at that time, the evidence didn't point to Carl's dystopian vision.

> **In evidence-based investing, decisions are based on well-documented research.**

The global economy is resilient. It has come through wars, market meltdowns, terrorist attacks, and other crises. Trade and commerce are alive and well and will continue as long as civilization persists. If civilization ceases, I'm guessing that the state of your investment accounts won't be top of mind.

And I said as much to Carl. I presented a more realistic view of an economy that would recover and thrive. He didn't believe me. His prophecy did not come true. In fact, on the whole, those investors who had laid out a reasonable strategy tailored to their situation and stuck with it through those years fared well.

The US recession lasted only a few years, followed by one of the longest expansions in history. Those who bailed out at the bottom in a panic were the big losers. However, because so many factors play a role, it can be next to impossible to guess the right time to invest or divest. You might expect a market plunge and along comes a rally, or vice versa. If you are going with your gut on when to buy and sell and trying to time the market, you're likely to do both at the wrong time. Instead, you need as many facts as you can muster.

Evidence-based investing means choosing your securities wisely and strategically, not emotionally.

Let's Get Real about Investing

The number one question people ask when they come to me for advice is this: "Where should I invest?" To which I can only say, "I don't know."

Don't get me wrong. I know plenty about investing, including the fact that I cannot competently advise someone I have just met. First, I find out about the new client's personal and family situation and other information I need to understand before I can answer what seemed like a simple question. In fact, the hard part is not picking the investments. That's easy. What's difficult is matching the investments to the individual and family. Thus, a great investment for you might be a terrible one for your neighbor.

Here is one example: What is your tax situation? That will be among the many variables determining whether an investment is right for you. Whether the

> **A great investment for you might be a terrible one for your neighbor.**

investment is taxable also will have much to do with its true performance. Never forget that. In a regular, taxable account, the government wants a cut of anything you make in the year that you earn it. Even if you are investing in a tax-sheltered environment such as a 401(k), the government will be claiming its due when you take out the money. Keep that in mind when designing your plan and look for tax efficient investments to keep your money growing as long as possible. (We will explore tax matters in Chapter 11.)

As you can see, it is difficult to come up with generic advice on investments that work for everyone. At BlueSky, we recommend a specific process for determining where to invest, and the first step is to realistically project the returns you can anticipate for different types of assets. Through the years, those asset classes have exhibited an expected rate of return, so you can reasonably estimate how they will perform for you, starting in the current economic climate and on into the future. You won't know the specific return in any given year, but over time, the average becomes more predictable.

BLUESKY LONG-TERM ASSET CLASS PLANNING ESTIMATES

ASSET CLASSES	ESTIMATED RETURN
FIXED INCOME	
US Treasury Bills	2.1
Intermediate-Term US Treasury Notes	3.9
Long-Term US Treasury Bonds	4.5
Long-Term Treasury Inflation-Protected Securities (TIPS)	4.6
Government Mortgage-Backed Securities	4.4
Intermediate-Term Municipal Bonds	3.6
Intermediate-Term Investment-Grade Corporate Bonds	4.6
Long-Term Investment-Grade Corporate Bonds	5.3
High-Yield Corporate Bonds	6.1
Foreign Government Bonds (Unhedged)	4.4
EQUITIES	
US Large-Cap Stocks	7.0
US Small-Cap Stocks	7.3
US Small-Value Stocks	7.8
Real Estate Investment Trusts (REITs)	6.8
Developed Countries Large-Cap Stocks	7.4
Developed Countries (Small Company)	7.7
Developed Countries (Small-Value Companies)	8.2
Emerging Market Stocks	9.1

Investing can get overly complicated. It need not be so. Once you have set your goals and established your personal investment policy statement, as we discussed in the previous chapter, it's time to get down to the details of designing your portfolio, basing decisions on the best available evidence.

"If I could just make twenty percent on my money, I'd be happy," people occasionally tell me. It's time to get real. A return that high can be possible for some business owners or for investors with expertise in a niche, but do not expect it in a standard stock or bond portfolio. It would entail high risk. You aren't playing the slots here. Even if you do have such a tolerance for risk, your expectations must be based on something other than wishful thinking.

Consider the historical market returns and the current realities of the markets. For example, as I write this, I'd expect that over the next ten to fifteen years, bonds will yield no more than 3-4 percent in the high-quality portion of the market. The stock market will be in the 6-7 percent range, much lower than historical returns. In your investment strategy and your plan, make sure your expectations are reasonable.

Your Mix of Stocks and Bonds

A key investment decision that will determine long-term success or failure will be how much of your portfolio you devote to equities and how much to fixed income—in other words, the percentage split between stocks and bonds.

With stocks, you have ownership. Your shares may go up in value and yield a dividend, but you have no guarantee of return. With bonds, you can get that guarantee. Essentially, you are lending your money to the government or to a corporation with the promise of getting a stated return and your principal back after a designated period. As long as the bond issuer is financially stable, your investment is guaranteed. Despite the current budget and deficit concerns, US Treasury bonds are still considered the safest asset class in the world. By comparison, bonds issued by a startup company will be much riskier.

> **Historically, equities have had better returns, but that potential for greater growth comes with much wider fluctuations in value as well as a an uncertainty of short-term returns. Bonds have had a much more certain return.**

How you split your money between equity and fixed income will largely determine your overall return and risk profile. If your investments are broadly diversified, you should get a reasonable return. Historically, equities have had better returns, but that potential for greater growth comes with much wider fluctuations in value as well as an uncertainty of short-term returns. Bonds have had a much more certain return. You get regular interest payments, either monthly, quarterly, or annually, and you get your principal back at the end of the fixed period.

The first step in designing a portfolio is to determine the percentages to allocate to stocks and bonds. For example, a 60/40 mix is 60 percent in stocks and 40 percent in bonds.

Stock Choices

As you diversify your equities, you can invest in an array of stock types, and you can also take a global perspective. Just under half the world's stocks come from companies headquartered in the United States and are subject to the US dollar, the US taxation system, and US regulatory bodies. Wise investors around the world invest in the equities of a variety of countries, including emerging ones. In the 1800s, the United States would have been considered an emerging market. Today, China, India, Russia, and Brazil are considered emerging. These countries are more volatile than they have been. But they will also be an important part of the future global economy, providing opportunities for higher returns. The point is: *think globally.*

Also make sure you are diversified by company size. Evidence suggests smaller companies can offer a higher expected return than big ones. Why? Because they act with more risk. Investing in a small or new company such as Keysight Technologies or Atmos Energy Corp (two randomly picked, small-cap companies) will be much riskier than investing in an established company such as Apple, Coca Cola, or Exxon. It's not that the more established companies present no risk. However, you would expect the smaller companies to have a higher risk and higher expected return.

Profitability matters too. Evidence shows that profitable companies exhibit higher long-term returns.

The stock of growth companies and value companies are two primary types of equities that could play a significant role in your portfolio.

Growth companies often make the headlines; think Google, Amazon, and Facebook in 2018. These are the companies whose revenue and/or earnings are booming, with great prospects for future growth. Other growth stocks have fantastic prospects but are actually losing money. For example, Tesla has been selling more cars, but its expenses are growing as fast as, if not faster than, sales. Hence, the company is burning cash. Uber is another example. The company borrows money or gets investor money to stay in business but doesn't make a profit. They are popular and exciting to talk about—and, typically, overpriced. You pay a premium to invest in these companies.

Value companies are less popular, even boring. Currently, Johnson & Johnson or AT&T would be considered value companies. Often, people have never heard of them or might groan at the mention of them. Their growth is sluggish, and their prospects seem uncertain at best. Some are teetering on collapse. Their stock sells at a discount. During the last recession, Ford was considered a value company. People thought it was going out of business, and the share price was cheap compared to the dividends it paid, its earnings, and the value of the assets it owned.

Value companies can serve your portfolio well if you buy in large numbers and diversify across economic sectors. Value equities have, historically, offered better returns over the long term than growth investments. Essentially, that is because when you buy into a value company, you get the stock at a bargain price that can grow to a premium. Conversely, when you buy into a growth company, you pay a premium that, most of the time, will shrink to a discounted price later.

Bond Choices

When investing in bonds, you should also diversify globally. As you do, a key question will be whether to purchase relatively safer government-issued bonds or earn a bit more income from slightly riskier corporate bonds.

A government, generally, has control over its currency, which means the risk of default is low because it prints more money to pay you back. However, if you are paid back with depreciated money, those bonds are not truly risk-free: you have lost purchasing power.

Among corporate bonds, the risk depends on the quality of the issuer. Smaller companies, particularly ones with questionable finances, will pay you a higher return on their bonds than big ones because they are riskier, which is why they're often called junk bonds. For that amount of risk, however, we are likely to recommend forgoing the junk bonds and investing your funds in the stock market where potential returns are much higher. Just keep your bond portfolio relatively boring.

Treasury inflation protected securities (TIPS) are a fairly new type of bond. These are mostly government bonds, though some companies have experimented with the concept.

Essentially, as an investor in TIPS, you get your stated rate of return with an adjustment to your principal each year to account for inflation. For example, say you invest in a $10,000 TIPS bond that pays a coupon of 1.5 percent. In the next year, inflation is 2 percent. You would collect your 1.5 percent on an additional 2 percent of principal, or $10,200. Because TIPS cannot fall behind inflation, they are a good investment to include in your bond portfolio.

When investing in bonds, consider the maturity of the bond or its *duration*.

Maturity is simply the time at which you will receive your principal back, whereas duration is a slightly more complicated calculation of the weighted average period before the cash flows involved are received. You don't get the full face value of a zero-coupon bond until the date of maturity, but if your bond pays annual coupons, you will recoup the cost of your investment somewhat sooner.

As a rule, the longer your money is tied up, the higher the interest rates. A thirty-year bond, for example, pays more than a one-year bond. I do not usually recommend long-dated bonds for the individual investor. Insurance companies and pension funds, as a rule, buy them to cover their obligations and long-term liabilities. However, individuals should buy most of their bonds with a recoup range of five to ten years (or shorter), depending on the investor's goals and the interest-rate environment.

> **A lot can happen over the decades, so don't be stuck with a bond that doesn't mature for a long time.**

A lot can happen over the decades, so don't be stuck with a bond that doesn't mature for a long time.

Rebalancing Your Portfolio

After you decide on the ratio of stocks and bonds in your portfolio and which investments to include in the various asset classes, then periodically rebalance your portfolio to keep it aligned with your goals.

For example, You may have originally decided on a 50/50 mix of stocks and bonds, but after a rally of several years, your stock holdings will have likely claimed an increasingly larger share of the overall portfolio. To stay true to your plan, you need to find a way to rebalance those levels.

How often you rebalance can be based on either the calendar or on your risk tolerance level. Some investors rebalance whenever their risk level gets too far from the plan. Some rebalance their portfolio every quarter or every year. The evidence is mixed on which period is preferable. Doing it too often can incur capital gains. Therefore, if your portfolio is in a tax-advantaged account, you might rebalance more often. If it is in a taxable account, then rebalancing too often can trigger unnecessary taxes.

Rebalancing can be a strategy either to reduce risk, enhance your return, or both.

> **To rebalance is a wise strategy. You show the discipline to sell high and buy low, and that's how to make money.**

As the value of stocks rises, you may periodically sell off some stocks and buy bonds. You might have achieved a higher return if you had kept all that money in stocks, but you wouldn't have been maintaining the level of risk and reward appropriate for you.

To rebalance is a wise strategy. You show the discipline to sell high and buy low, and that's how to make money.

Pooled Investment Vehicles

I used to invest in individual securities, but much has changed over the years. This kind of trading doesn't offer enough reward for the risk taken in today's hypertrading world.

Just as there's no evidence that fund managers can beat the market over the long term, there's no evidence that buying individual stocks will do so, either. It's tempting to think you can find the next big winner the way some found Amazon or Microsoft. Remember, hindsight is 20/20.

While it's fun to think you can determine the future winners in the stock market, you pay an opportunity cost in trying to pick, for example, Coke versus Pepsi, Exxon versus Mobil, or Apple versus Google. In reality, the best returns will be achieved by *owning all of them*. I suggest that rather than picking individual investments, you own your stocks and bonds through a mutual fund or an exchange traded fund (ETF). These are called pooled investment vehicles because your money is lumped with other investors. You gain the advantage of being able to buy into a wide variety of securities at a lower cost and in a more convenient format.

> **Just as there's no evidence that fund managers can beat the market over the long term, there's no evidence that buying individual stocks will do so, either.**

With a passive (index) mutual fund, you give your money to an intermediary company that buys a predetermined basket of stocks or bonds, seeking to meet the fund's stated investment objectives. You own a proportional share of the fund itself rather than the actual underlying investments. Be aware, however, that the actions of other investors in the fund can influence your returns. Let's say there are one hundred investors in a mutual fund and 99 of them decide to sell their shares in the fund. The fund manager has to sell the securities in the fund, leaving you (the only remaining owner) to bear a lot of the tax cost of the sales made by the other investors.

With an ETF, the purchase of shares of individual stocks or bonds is handled in a similar way. It's done according to a predetermined allocation and held at the intermediary company on your behalf. For accounting purposes, though, you are not lumped in with the other investors in the ETF. Your purchases and sales have no impact on them, nor do their transactions have a tax consequence for you. If you want your money back from an ETF, the fund does not have to sell other investors' shares.

Think of it this way: your mutual fund investments are like the ingredients in one big pie that everyone shares. Investors in an exchange traded fund, on the other hand, have their own individual pies made of the same ingredients as everyone else's. If fellow investors sell their pie, nothing happens to yours.

When you are ready to invest, you can choose from among many good mutual funds and ETFs from several reputable fund companies. I recommend looking for low-cost investments in broadly diversified funds that track large assets classes. Stay away from narrowly defined funds that track, say, a specific industry or a small country. Instead, choose funds that have a track record of meeting their objectives.

The graphs on the following page explain the difference between ETFs and Mutual Funds.

ETFs VS. MUTUAL FUNDS

ETFs

☑ Tax advantage due to internal trades conducted with shares rather than cash, resulting in fewer capital gains taxes.

☑ Traded on exchanges.

☑ Priced by supply and demand of traders, varying through the trading day.

☑ Managed by an ETF sponsor, usually following an index, and an authorized participant with the help of a trust.

☑ Charge management fees.

☑ Contain a variety of underlying securities.

☑ Must be registered with the Securities and Exchange Commission in the USA.

MUTUAL FUNDS

- ☑ Often sells underlying securities for cash, putting a tax burden on all shareholders.

- ☑ Transactions take place between the investors and the fund itself.

- ☑ Price is set at the end of the trading day based on the value of individual investments in the fund.

- ☑ Managed by a registered investment advisor and overseen by a board of directors or board of trustees.

- ☑ Charge management fees.

- ☑ Contain a variety of underlying securities.

- ☑ Must be registered with the Securities and Exchange Commission in the USA.

Investing for Life

You want more than just a grab bag of investments. Ideally, your investments meet your goals and serve your purpose, taking on only as much risk as necessary to do so. Deciding on the mix of stocks and bonds in your portfolio will probably be your most important decision, so make sure those percentages remain in alignment with your financial plan from year to year.

Don't invest as if you were gambling. Rather, invest realistically and dispassionately in full knowledge of the likely returns your investments will generate. Feel free to use our estimates from this chapter. Companies such as Vanguard and Charles Schwab & Co. also create estimates of future returns. You should not guess; you should know. Thus, you can base your expectations on sound research, guided by the principles of evidence-based investing.

Remember, the reason you are investing is to achieve your life goals. If you have taken the time to develop a comprehensive plan, you already know the cost of your goals

You should not guess; you should know.

and when you intend to achieve them. With that firmly in mind, it should be relatively easy to choose the right investments to accomplish them.

My friend Carl was sincere but misinformed in his vision of economic doom. As long as people need goods and services, economies will endure. They will endure as long as people aspire to profit from their labors and initiatives.

Investing is nothing new. In history, the Spanish royals financed Christopher Columbus's bold venture in 1492 in hopes of a golden return on investment. Investors have traded in corporate and government securities for hundreds of years since. Never mind the sooth-sayers and doomsayers and the commentators du jour. If you believe that human ingenuity is ending, then don't invest at all. Otherwise, let the markets themselves carry you to where you want to go.

The markets have served investors well for generations, and they will do so for generations to come.

CHAPTER 8

BEWARE OF ALTERNATIVE INVESTMENTS

Beyond the familiar world of stocks, bonds, and real estate is the realm of alternative investments: hedge funds, gold, private equity, and even strategies that try to win by betting against success. Proceed with great caution.

razilian cherry wood? Hey, it just might be the next big thing, the opportunity of a lifetime! This actually was one of the ventures under discussion when I became chairman of a hospital system's investment committee. I was dismayed to see that the system's financial advisor, a big brokerage firm, had loaded the hospital's portfolio with hedge funds and alternative investments.

Wall Street seems to have become enamored with alternatives. Investors have been rushing blindly to get in on the latest fad rather than hold on to those plain old boring stocks and bonds. Instead of looking for reliable performers, they are knocking on wood (and lots of other fancy stuff), hoping to cash in on risky bets.

Many institutions and high-net-worth investors have been lured into the alternatives trap. To rationalize their adventurous escapades, they often point to high historical returns earned by the Harvard University endowment fund. If the alternatives work for such a hallowed institution, they reason, they should work for everyone.

Here's the truth: they won't. A high return on alternatives is the exception rather than the rule. And if you take a closer look, you will see that Harvard and some of the other large funds that started the trend have significantly pulled back their investments in alternatives. It's a losing strategy.

One gentleman recently asked me to take over the management of his investments, telling me he had lost money in 2017. How could an investor possibly lose money in a year like 2017 when the US stock market gained approximately 20 percent? I looked at his portfolio. Ninety percent of it was in hedge funds.

What Is an Alternative Investment?

Alternative investments are outside the familiar world of stocks, bonds, and real estate. They include currencies, commodities (e.g., oil and gas), natural gas futures, cattle futures, and metals (gold, silver, platinum). Collectibles such as wine, art, and classic cars also can be alternative investments. Although some people do think of real estate as an alternative investment, I consider it to be its own unique class.

Often, alternative investments are found within a container such as a hedge fund. The investment may be a managed future, such as a stock or commodity future, for which you pay today for the right to obtain the asset later.

Traditionally, alternative investments have been illiquid, tying up investors' money for extended periods. Wall Street firms have packaged alternatives into mutual funds so they are liquid and can be traded as stocks and bonds can, but the hefty fees for that convenience wipe out any investment advantage, if one even exists.

Offering the prospect of a higher return than stocks or bonds, a lot of the alternatives came into prominence after the global financial crisis. Awakened to the risks of the stock market, many investors looked to the alternatives, hoping for a rate of return that would not subject them to the potential of a market collapse. Alternatives were viewed as an opportunity to diversify. If the markets were going down, the alternative investments might be going up, giving the investors a smoother ride—or so they thought. In reality, a lot of alternative investments simply are not worth the risk.

Let's take a look now at three of the alternatives in which investors are often tempted to partake: hedge funds, gold, and private equity.

Hedge Funds

Many people think of hedge funds as synonymous with alternative investments. Hedge funds actually are containers that can include alternatives as well as regular stocks and bonds. The alternative nature of a hedge fund lies in the innovative strategies for investing those underlying assets.

For example, the fund may buy some stocks "long" (which is standard investing, betting they will rise in value) while "shorting" other stocks (which is betting they will fall in value).[2] Hedge funds

---

2   When you buy long, you purchase a share and own it, and if the price rises, you win. When you short a stock, you borrow it, and if the price rises, you lose. Here's how it works: the market allows you to trade stocks that you do not own, borrowing them from a broker to return later. Let's say you borrow a share and sell it right away for the going price of $10, hoping the price will then fall. Why? Because you must buy it back so you can return it to the broker. If you can buy it back for, say, $8, you get to pocket $2. However, let's say you guess wrong, sell the share for $10, and then the price rises to $12. Now, you have to pay an extra $2 to repurchase the share so you can return it (at a loss to you of $2 per share).

also engage in arbitrage. An example of arbitrage is when a fund buys dollars on one exchange and sells euros on another exchange in an attempt to take advantage of currency price differentials.

Contrary to general expectations, some hedge funds do have good track records. The huge Renaissance Technologies hedge fund company is one. Before it closed to new investors, its flagship Medallion Fund's minimum buy-in was out of reach for most investors, and in fact, most of the money in the fund is from the founder and the employees.

Most hedge funds with the greatest returns are closed or don't accept money from new investors. Mediocre hedge funds need to attract a lot of investors to make money because they are not making it from their strategy. In other words, the best ones don't want your money—you *can't* get in—while the weak ones do want your money, but you *shouldn't* get in. Hedge funds often charge exceedingly high fees, so as a general rule, I advise against investing in them.

A strategy that looks for market inefficiencies can succeed only as long as few investors have identified those opportunities. Once people catch on to the "secret" and duplicate the arbitrage, the opportunity gradually disappears. If you are investing a lot of money, most strategies will not work for you. You will be far better off with the traditional asset classes and strategies. Think of the housing market in your neighborhood or small community. Some homes may be underpriced and good deals, but if a large firm with billions of dollars were to come in and buy up the housing stock, your neighborhood soon would have no underpriced homes. It's the law of supply and demand.

There has been a mass exodus from hedge funds recently. Endowments, pension funds, and other entities that invested in hedge funds are realizing they don't have access to the top-tier managers, or even if they do, the investment is not worth the fees and mediocre returns. For example, the California Public Employees' Retirement System (CalPERS), the largest pension system in the world, has drastically cut back on its use of hedge funds over the past several years. Harvard and Yale also have reduced their use of them.

Years ago, David Swensen, who once ran the Yale Endowment Fund, wrote a book for institutional investors titled *Pioneering Portfolio Management*, based on the Yale Endowment Fund model. Individual investors were interested in it, so he wrote another book, basically telling them, "Don't try this at home, folks." In *Unconventional Success: A Fundamental Approach to Personal Investment*, Swensen recommends staying with more traditional investments.

> **There has been a mass exodus from hedge funds recently. Endowments, pension funds, and other entities that invested in hedge funds are realizing they don't have access to the top-tier managers, or even if they do, the investment is not worth the fees and mediocre returns.**

Gold

Many people believe that gold is a great hedge against inflation, while others hold to the theory that it is a solid investment that will protect them in the event of total currency collapse. Both are flawed perspectives.

When you compare the rise and fall of gold prices through the years with the year-to-year changes in the inflation rate, there is no discernible correlation. The returns from gold appear to have no relationship to inflation. Though many investors assume that gold prices rise during times of inflation, no clear relationship exist. Rather, it's more like this: *Gold prices rise when gold prices rise. Investors buy more of it when they see an upswing.*

The price of gold is driven by speculation, and at times, the price has been fixed or dictated by the government, not the free market. Private ownership of gold was even outlawed by US President Franklin Roosevelt in 1933 and not made legal again until 1974.[3]

As for those who believe gold will serve them well in the event of a global currency crisis or during some apocalypse of their imagination, let me ask this: If our society and economy were to collapse into utter chaos, if a bear market were to get so bad that we traded in bearskins, do you really think those gold coins in your safe deposit box would help you much? In a world like that, you would need more than gold to protect you. You would not be swapping bags of nuggets for provisions to take to your hillside cave. I've been in war-torn countries where society has essentially collapsed, and people aren't running around with bags of gold to buy food at the grocery store.

It comes down to this: investing most of your money in gold is generally a bad idea. If it makes you feel better to collect some Krugerrands, go for it, but don't go too far. I had an elderly client whose previous financial manager had invested most of her money in gold, which meant she missed the entire bull market of the 1990s. Gold has had its run-ups from time to time, but it's just not reliable

---

3   Daniel Fisher, "Gold: Not Much Of A Hedge For Anything, Unless You're A Centurion," *Forbes*, August 8, 2013, https://www.forbes.com/sites/daniel-fisher/2013/08/08/gold-not-much-of-a-hedge-for-anything-unless-youre-a-centurion/#815fd196a744.

enough an investment to hold in great quantities. Don't let the glitter blind you.

Private Equity

The world of private equity encompasses a wide range of options, most of which involve investing in companies that are not publicly traded. If you intend to invest this way, look for opportunities in areas where you have specialized knowledge or can become part owner of a business. Beware of the packaged products from Wall Street that can get into private equity funds laden with fees yet producing mediocre returns.

> **Gold has had its run-ups from time to time, but it's just not reliable enough an investment to hold in great quantities. Don't let the glitter blind you.**

If you want to invest directly in a private company, carefully evaluate whether you are looking at a good opportunity. That calls for due diligence, even when the company is owned by someone in your family. Some people of retirement age feel confident in investing in their children's companies as a way to diversify while supporting a family endeavor. That can be risky, but if the company is healthy and growing, the investment could be a valuable addition to a portfolio— as long as it's kept to a small percentage.

One of my clients owned a large farm, and one of his crops was cotton. A group of investors put together an opportunity for him to own a portion of the cotton gin that processed some of the cotton. He didn't run the company. He wasn't the owner at the decision-making level of management, but he put some money into the company and received a share of the profits. Moreover, he had some expertise in this area and could properly evaluate the opportunity. This is a good example of how private equity need not be overly fancy or complicated.

Another client moved to eastern North Carolina near our offices by the ocean. He was retired, had some money, and was interested in private equity. He wanted to own some type of business, but he didn't want it to be a full-time job. He found a surf shop at the beach that was open only three months a year. I helped him evaluate the deal. He was able to become a part owner and have some say in the management of the business. It wasn't a full-time job; it was a financial investment—another low-key way to become involved in private equity.

Seldom Worth the Risk

So, what's the bottom line on investing in alternatives?

I do not recommend it, with the exception of private equity, and even then, only when it's narrowly defined. Here's the problem with alternatives: as a rule, the fees will be high and the returns will be low or not what you expected. Nor are you likely to get the diversification benefit you need. Mainly you face high risk while tying up your money.

Remember, to meet your goals you must be able to reliably predict the kind of returns you are likely to get. That is difficult to do with alternatives.

A good mix of stocks, bonds, and real estate is a better way to stay on course. Investors often come to me with a variety of choices they are considering, and I help analyze them. We identify goals and values and then find investments that would be more suitable than the alternatives. When we do go the alternative route, we are not looking to invest in hedge funds—most of them have dismal records—or managed futures, or mutual funds in the alternative space. We stay away from Wall Street's prepackaged products laden with fees. Instead, we look for something that would be a good fit for the investor's niche or expertise. Only then does it make sense to invest in alternatives.

> **So, what's the bottom line on investing in alternatives?**
> **I do not recommend it, with the exception of private equity, and even then, only when it's narrowly defined.**

Anyone interested in alternatives should seek sober professional guidance. Never mind the parade of TV financial shows with one fast talker after another ballyhooing a hedge fund or failsafe investment or proprietary strategy. If you don't know what you are doing, you are courting trouble.

People are now buzzing about bitcoins, the digital currency that has attracted offbeat investors who seem destined to go bust. The hype can go far astray of common sense. Don't wish upon a falling star!

CHAPTER 9

INVESTING IN PROPERTY

Real estate can be a great way to diversify a portfolio. As with any investment, however, there is a right way and a wrong way to go about it. Purchasing and managing properties aren't for everybody, but you still can get a piece of the action.

After emigrating from Ireland, Mary pursued the American dream in multiples. She had a great job with a major corporation and, through the years, she lived in various places up and down the East Coast. Mary had heard over and over that the smart money was in real estate, so she bought into it—in fact, six times. Wherever her career took her, she purchased a single-family home and kept it as a rental property.

Mary had gotten caught up in the euphoria of the robust property markets of the mid-2000s, and she wasn't actually evaluating those houses as investments. She came to see me after the housing bubble burst. I looked at her tax returns, and we calculated the income for each of the properties minus the expenses for mortgages and repairs. They were difficult for her to manage because they were all over the map. She was losing money on all of them.

Over the next several years, I helped Mary sell those properties to rid herself of a big headache and a big risk. IRS rules prevented her from deducting the losses against her high income, but the rules also allow the losses to be "suspended" (accumulated) until they can be used to offset a permissible capital gain or when a property is disposed of. As it turned out, the company where Mary worked was sold. As a shareholder, she realized a multimillion-dollar gain, and we were able to time the sale of her properties to offset a substantial amount of the taxes on that gain.

Nothing in the world of investments is failsafe, despite what you might hear on a late-night infomercial. Making assumptions is a good way to deplete a portfolio. Mary's mistake—one people often make whether acquiring real estate or any other type of investment—was not having a strategy. She plunked down her money without a plan.

A Place in Your Portfolio?

Real estate can be lucrative for those who know how to find the good deals or invest with those who do. However, tracking how much money you are making (if you're making any at all) can be difficult. If you own shares in XYZ Corp., you will know how much it gained or lost in the previous year. No such specific return is posted for real estate. I have found that, most of the time, people are unaware what they are making is quite modest, considering the amount of hassle and risk they incur.

Homeowners often glow with pride as they talk about how much more the house is worth than when they bought it a decade earlier. However, they aren't factoring in their monthly mortgage payments all those years, or those annual property tax bills, or how much they shelled out for repairs and renovations. They would be chagrined to discover what they thought was a big gain may be little or nothing; it could very well amount to a loss.

First and foremost, your house is a place to live. If you make money on it, that's great, but don't let the National Association of Realtors convince you it's an investment.

First and foremost, your house is a place to live. If you make money on it, that's great, but don't let the National Association of Realtors convince you it's an investment.

Nonetheless, homeownership can be highly beneficial for a variety of reasons, one of which is the deduction for mortgage interest and property tax payments. The government has long provided that tax break as a means to encourage people to purchase a residence, recognizing that the pride of ownership helps communities prosper.

Among the provisions of the new tax law signed by President Donald Trump in December 2017 is the limitation, to a total of $10,000 per taxpayer, set on deductions for real estate and other taxes. For new mortgages, the mortgage interest deduction is limited to $750,000 of debt. For home equity loans, interest is deductible only on money borrowed to buy, build, or improve the home. Fortunately, married couples can still get a capital gains exclusion of $500,000 (or $250,000 for a single person) on the sale of a primary residence.

A fixed-rate mortgage is also an effective hedge against inflation. When I was a child, my parents bought a home with a traditional thirty-year mortgage at a fixed rate of interest. Years later, after I had moved away, they mentioned they had paid off that mortgage. Through the years, month by month, they had sent in the same amount. Inflation was raising the cost of living by at least a few percent annually, but their payment stayed the same. At the end, they were paying half what many people spend each month on a car payment. When inflation is rearing, borrowing money at a fixed rate can be a sensible strategy.

Investment properties, likewise, can help round out a portfolio, but caution is always in order. They, too, can produce disappointing returns once expenses are calculated. Whenever I ask real estate investors about their rate of return, they usually say something like, "Well, I bought it for $300,000, and it's worth $400,000 now." That's not a rate of return. That's just how much the property's market value went up, or how much the owner imagines it went up. The investor could have done just as well, and perhaps better, by purchasing Treasury bills and sitting on the sofa to watch TV, with none of the troubles of dealing with surly tenants and leaking roofs.

If you are looking to buy real estate as an investment and not as your home, you should identify properties that can give you a strong cash flow with a minimum of risk and management trouble.

My philosophy is that if you are looking to buy real estate as an investment and not as your home, you should identify properties that can give you a strong cash flow with a minimum of risk and management trouble.

Before you buy, always make sure the numbers will work for you, and consider all the expenses that will be

REAL ESTATE INVESTING CONTINUUM

OWN AND MANAGE LOCAL PROPERTY	HIRED MANAGEMENT, TURNKEY PROPERTIES	SYNDICATED PROPERTIES	PRIVATE REITs	INDIVIDUAL PUBLIC REITs	REIT MUTUAL FUND

Higher Possible Returns

Average Market Returns

MOST EXPERIENCE REQUIRED
MOST HASSLE
LEAST DIVERSIFICATION
LEAST LIQUIDITY
MOST CONTROL
MORE TAX BENEFITS
FEWEST LAYERS OF FEES

LEAST EXPERIENCE REQUIRED
LEAST HASSLE
MOST DIVERSIFICATION
MOST LIQUIDITY
LEAST CONTROL
LESS TAX BENEFITS
MOST LAYERS OF FEES

associated with your ownership. An investment should bring you an immediate and regular return. If you base your decision to purchase on your expectation that eventually it will appreciate in value, that is called speculation. You will still have expenses along the way, but the property will not be giving you an income to cover them.

While there's nothing evil about speculating, I prefer to invest in real estate for cash flow with the possibility of appreciation, rather than no income and a hope that the price will go up.

How to Invest in Real Estate

Getting involved in real estate investment does not necessarily mean you need to be dealing directly with bricks and mortar. Let's look at several approaches to take advantage of opportunities in the real estate market. I have arranged them in order of the easiest to most difficult. In some ways, it's also a ladder of risk. You should never imagine that you can eliminate risk altogether.

Factors to consider for each, besides the level of risk, are the potential return, price volatility, management responsibility, the debt load, tax issues, and liquidity.

REITS, PUBLIC AND PRIVATE

The easiest way to add property to your portfolio with the least amount of hassle and principal risk is to purchase shares in a public real estate investment trust (REIT).

A REIT is a company that owns and manages commercial properties producing income. They could be apartment buildings, shopping malls, office complexes, and hospitals. Some REITs also produce income by investing in mortgages. A public REIT is registered with the US Securities and Exchange Commission (SEC) and is traded on a major exchange as a stock is.

This means as an individual investor, you can become a part owner, albeit a miniscule-part owner, of a portfolio of buildings. It can be as easy as the click of a mouse.

A REIT usually specializes in a specific sector of real estate or specific region or country. You can buy into a health care REIT, for example, or an office REIT. Most REITs build their portfolio by buying and operating properties and collecting rent. The REIT is required by law to distribute at least 90 percent of its taxable income to its shareholders as dividends.

With a REIT, you gain the advantage of liquidity that's often missing when directly buying and selling real estate. If you need your money, you can click the mouse again and sell your shares. In addition, you are not taking on the risk of borrowing money. Thus, a REIT is an easy entry into real estate investment. Once again, however, there is no guarantee. The shares are subject to ups and downs as stocks are and particularly as interest rates rise and fall.

A private REIT has the same structure as a public REIT but is not traded on an exchange. It is not regulated by the SEC, and it is likely to be riskier. Before handing over your money, look closely at the fees and terms. In the 1980s, these were sold as tax shelters, but tax laws are not eternal, and when the IRS eliminated the tax advantage, investors were stuck with shares that nobody seemed to want anymore. To make matters worse, they ended up with big tax bills.

> **A REIT is an easy entry into real estate investment. Once again, however, there is no guarantee.**

Despite the potential greater risk, there are, nonetheless, some excellent private REITs available. You can invest to own a portion of a portfolio of properties without saddling yourself with responsibility for the debt or the property management. You benefit from the income, and, if the REIT is sold, you also benefit from any capital gains.

Often, private REITs offer the opportunity for greater cash flow, but their biggest advantage is this: because they don't publicly trade, they aren't subject to wide market fluctuations or panic selling.

PRIVATE SPONSOR-LED INVESTMENTS

Next on the ladder are my favorite type of real estate investments, private sponsor-led investments.

Unlike REITs, which function more as stocks do, these investments are structured so you become a part-owner of the properties through a limited partnership (LP) or a limited liability company (LLC). This is a more direct form of ownership than a REIT.

At tax time, you file a Schedule K1 to report your share of the partnership's income and deductions rather than filing a simple dividend report.

Private investments of this type can involve extensive holdings or may be relatively small local deals in which the sponsor finds and buys properties and provides professional management. The investors are not asked to guarantee the loans, which is a major advantage over the next two types of ownership.

The returns can be much better for this style of investment, and the tax structure is also advantageous. You have opportunities for Section 1031 tax-free exchanges, in which you can defer capital gains taxes when a property is sold and you reinvest the money in another property within a certain time limit.

Generally, you cannot do that with REITs. However, as I have emphasized repeatedly, you must know what you are getting into. These are private investments. You and your advisor should examine every word of the agreements.

SMALL GROUP INVESTMENT

While *small group investment* is not a technical term, there is no other way to describe it than an arrangement in which a small group comes together to buy a building. To do so, the group will structure a simple partnership or a limited liability company that will own it.

If you join in such an endeavor, you may have to take on some of the management responsibilities, such as finding and screening tenants, and you will be sharing financial risk with the others in the small group. Usually, you will be liable for the debt.

DIRECT OWNERSHIP

Becoming the direct owner of real estate entails a greater amount of risk, although you could also get a higher return. You are buying into a lot of work and responsibility. It will be your job to identify a good deal on a property that will produce a reliable income, finance the purchase, and manage the mortgage, find suitable tenants who will pay on time and treat your property well, collect the rent, and keep up with all the maintenance and any improvements that might be necessary.

Which Way Is Best for You?

Many people jump right to the direct ownership approach of real estate investment because they don't realize they could get involved in other ways and still get decent returns with fewer headaches and less risk.

As you decide whether to invest in real estate and how, ask yourself: "What do I know that others do not? What is my advantage over others?"

Becoming the direct owner of real estate entails a greater amount of risk, although you could also get a higher return.

For example, you may have an intimate understanding of your community, how it has evolved, and how it's likely to keep changing. Or you may have a proven instinct for financial deal making. If you cannot identify any personal advantage and simply want to include real estate in your portfolio as a means to diversify, then you likely will be better off avoiding direct ownership in favor of the REIT-type or sponsor-led investments.

The world of real estate can produce greater opportunities to exploit market inefficiencies than you are likely to discover in, say, the stock market, where pricing is instantaneous. With good old-fashioned legwork and investigation, you could uncover good deals and make them a valuable part of your portfolio. If you use debt prudently to finance those good deals, you can leverage your investment to even greater gains, or you can partner with a professional real estate investor to make it happen.

A good reason to include real estate in your portfolio is its tendency to provide an uncorrelated return. That is, it doesn't rise and fall in tandem with stocks or bonds. Even a bear market does not necessarily mean your real estate is declining. Regardless of what is happening in the markets, people still need a place to live and businesses need a place to operate. That makes real estate investment a great way to diversify your portfolio.

Residential and Commercial Options

Let's look in more detail at specific investments—namely, single-family residences, multiunit properties, and large commercial properties.

SINGLE-FAMILY RESIDENCES

Many investors wade into real estate by purchasing single-family residences, which is probably the worst way to start out. It's hard to make money that way, as the story starting this chapter illustrates. When you invest in a single-family home, you have one property with one tenant, and your efforts don't do much to diversify your portfolio.

Investors also tend to look for higher-priced homes, for which they can charge more rent. If you expect to be active in the single-family rental market, I recommend sticking to homes that most middle-class or lower-middle-class Americans can afford. Such properties are much easier to rent, but you need to have a good collections system in play.

I also recommend finding a high-quality property manager. You can do it yourself, and that's fine when everything is going smoothly. If you were to have one bad tenant and needed to proceed to an eviction, however, you might wish you had hired a good property manager to handle the details for you.

A good reason to include real estate in your portfolio is its tendency to provide an uncorrelated return. That is, it doesn't rise and fall in tandem with stocks or bonds.

Look for opportunities in areas where people are seeking a particular type of housing. Some investors look for houses at the beach or in the mountains and rent them as vacation properties. Others seek to tap into opportunities in college towns. If you have a child in college, consider buying a house or condo near the campus that your child can share with a couple of friends to cover the mortgage payments. If you know the parents of those friends, that arrangement could work well. Be careful, though, about bringing in random students as housemates. They might seem like fine young people but end up trashing the place.

MULTIUNIT PROPERTIES

Multiunit properties such as duplexes, quadraplexes, or small apartment buildings can be profitable investments. You can usually get better deals on larger properties that can accommodate more than a single family. You get some diversification, and you start to build scale with multiple streams of income from the building.

Mobile home parks can also be a good choice for investment. The cost is low, and the maintenance is usually relatively easy. If your area attracts good tenants, mobile home parks can be quite profitable.

At some point, you need to decide whether you want to be a passive investor in apartments or actively pursue this as part of your business. If you have the time and inclination to become involved, consider purchasing large buildings or complexes. Otherwise, limit yourself to a few apartments.

LARGE COMMERCIAL PROPERTIES

With large commercial properties, you often see what are called triple net leases or big box store leases. In those arrangements, you own the land and lease it to a large franchise chain, such as Walmart or Walgreens. The franchisee usually takes care of all the taxes, insurance, and maintenance on the buildings. Most leases will be for ten, twenty, or thirty years; franchise owners don't want to erect a building on land with only a short-term lease. As a real estate investment, this type of lease arrangement is lucrative. Although the return likely will be a little lower than you'd get from other forms of real estate investment, the risk is also generally lower.

If you want to buy individual commercial buildings on your own, consider those with service businesses that have minimal foot traffic. You will be taking on less liability risk that way. Also, doctors, lawyers, financial advisors, and other service professionals tend not to move out quickly. Once they have established the practice, they want to stay, which makes those buildings a stable investment. We caution people to avoid buying real estate that is home to startups, especially technology firms, because if their funding dries up, they might leave unexpectedly, and you're stuck. And think twice before buying buildings occupied by mom-and-pop shops, which tend to have a brief business lifespan.

If you are interested in investing in raw land for large commercial properties, be prepared for a ton of governmental red tape and environmental regulations. Trying to develop raw land can be a headache, so do your homework and get good advice so you can proceed competently and confidently.

Keeping Out of Trouble

Most of the time, you will be well served with real estate in your portfolio. To avoid many of the common pitfalls, however, limit your investments to the professionally managed, pooled type. Don't become the sole owner of properties unless you have a clear advantage and the time to devote to the effort.

Real estate investors often get into trouble because they over-leverage themselves. Along comes an adverse circumstance, and the tenant may no longer be able to pay the mortgage. A tenant also could file a lawsuit for injury, so make sure you have good liability protection.

Getting good advice is crucial. In mainstream financial circles, valuable strategies often go unspoken. Most advisers are paid on a percentage of the money that they manage, and since they don't manage real estate, they don't have much to say about it. In fact, most brokerage firms don't allow their advisors to talk to their clients about investing in real estate. It's not usually covered by their insurance, or their compliance departments won't let them, and they don't know anything about it anyway.

Instead, work with an advisor who can knowledgeably answer questions about the big decisions you must make:

- Is it time to refinance?

- Do you need to upgrade?

- Should you consider selling?

You need real answers to these real questions.

But if you do it right, real estate investing can yield returns higher than those usually seen in the equity markets. And if you have the stamina to stick with it, the rewards can be significant.

CHAPTER 10

YOUR GUARANTEED INCOME

As you plan your steps to financial independence, one element will be "guaranteed" income, or streams of money that you can be reasonably confident will continue. Examples include a pension, Social Security, and payments from an annuity.

Bill never had much money, so when the gas company offered him an early retirement package while he was in his fifties, he jumped for the lump sum instead of monthly pension payments. With half a million dollars in the bank, he felt like a rich man, and he proceeded to play the role. First, he paid off the house; it seemed like the right thing to do. Then he bought a shiny new pickup truck. His kids asked for handouts, so why not? He enjoyed feeling like the generous dad with deep pockets.

Soon enough, those pockets weren't so deep anymore. When he finally came to see me early in my career as a financial advisor, half of that money was gone. Frankly, there wasn't much I could do. For Bill, it was too late. Several of his coworkers had called me for advice when the gas company—Progress Energy, which bought out North Carolina Natural Gas—offered early retirement packages. They asked the right questions up front: Should I take the lump sum or the monthly pension? Or, if they already had chosen the lump sum: Can you help me invest this money, so it will last the rest of my life?

Bill had assumed that this manna from heaven would take care of him and his wife until the end of their days. Not so, and now they faced decades of financial struggle. Bill had developed no strategy and set no goals, letting much of the money slip away. At least his kids were grown and out of the house, no doubt happily spending the cash he had given them. There wasn't enough in the bank to pay the bills for long, and it would be years before Bill would be old enough to collect Social Security. His financial future was bleak.

As it turned out, he didn't have to struggle long. Bill's wife soon divorced him, and five years later, he died. That's not what you would call a happy ending, but at least it was an ending.

Now, I'm not suggesting that anyone in Bill's situation should always go for the monthly pension payments. Sometimes the lump sum is the smarter choice—that is, for those who have the discipline to handle a lot of money. They could self-annuitize the lump sum to produce an income potentially greater than the monthly benefit would have been, with more control over their assets and something to leave for their heirs. In the case of Progress Energy, the options were particularly generous on the lump-sum side, which was unusual. When we do the math, the monthly benefit is generally a better deal than the lump sum.

It comes down to an easy equation, comparing the lump sum with the annuity and figuring the implied rates of return.

Money, however, is about more than math. Bill made a sensible choice, technically, but he made the wrong choice for his situation. He wasn't equipped to manage money, and he lacked the wisdom to seek help. I learned long ago that the right decision has less to do with calculations and more to do with psychology, behavior, and personality. So many people come to me looking for the financial answer, when the answer lies within them. The "right" choice may not be the best choice.

Bill's best bet would have been to take his pension in the form of a monthly benefit. For thirty years, he had been accustomed to getting a paycheck. Now he needed a reliable flow of cash to replace those paychecks. He could have invested that lump sum to produce the income he needed, but he didn't know where to start. He didn't even know he was *supposed* to start.

A company pension is one example of so-called guaranteed income: a monthly stream of money that, presumably, will continue to come in regardless of any somersaults in the economy. Other examples are Social Security benefits and insurance annuities. In this chapter, we look at guaranteed income in its various forms.

Defined Benefit Plans

Whether to choose a lump sum or a monthly benefit has become a far less common question these days. Most companies have done away with the pensions that countless families once depended upon for retirement security. They have replaced those "defined benefit" plans with the ubiquitous "defined contribution" plans, the 401(k)-type programs that have come to dominate the retirement planning landscape since they were introduced in the 1980s. In effect, the move away from pensions put the responsibility for retirement planning squarely on the shoulders of the worker rather than the employer.

Except in the small-business arena, I'm not aware of any companies that are starting new defined benefit plans. Bigger companies are not, and only a few still offer them. A risk of the defined benefit plans is that they depend on the company's stability. Pension plans can go bankrupt, as many airline employees know so well. When a pension plan fails, it is taken over by the Pension Benefit Guaranty Corporation, which is funded by employers but backstopped by the government. For high earners, the pension benefit is capped: they get significantly lower monthly payments than they had expected.

For those who still do have a defined benefit plan, the company usually offers options: e.g., a lump sum, payments for life, smaller payments that will continue for a surviving spouse, or payments limited to a certain number of years. The best choice will depend on your family circumstances, so get qualified advice on how to proceed from a trusted advisor who knows you well.

Most federal, state, and municipal government plans offer you and/or your spouse a guaranteed income for life when you retire. The military also falls into that category. After twenty years of service, you can retire from the military and collect a paycheck for the rest of your life. As a rule, the benefit rises each year at the rate of inflation. Because the federal government can print money, you need not worry about the risk of default. However, there is some risk at the state and municipal level, as we have seen in high-profile cases in California, Illinois, and Detroit. There, benefits have been cut for future retirees. Federal government pensions, however, are likely to provide a secure income stream.

Social Security Benefits

The first question we need to ask about Social Security is whether it will be there for us. It's safe to say that unless society collapses, we will have some sort of benefit for people as they reach old age. Those who are fifty or older, or who are already retired, can expect their promised benefits to remain reasonably intact. However, as it stands, the Social Security system is unsustainable, and younger workers could see major changes.

The earliest you can claim Social Security benefits is age sixty-two, but you receive a reduced benefit if you choose early retirement. For people born between 1943 and 1954, the full retirement age is sixty-six. For people born between 1955 and 1960, it gradually increases to age sixty-seven. If you further postpone retirement, your monthly benefit will increase by about 8 percent every year you wait until it is capped at age seventy. So, if Fred waited until he reached seventy to claim a benefit, he would get 32 percent more each month than if he had filed his claim at his full retirement age of sixty-six.

As you get into your sixties, you have a decision to make, and many people make the wrong choice. If you retire at the age of sixty-two, your benefit reduction will be at least 25 percent, and you will be locked into that amount for the rest of your life. In addition, the amount you can earn from a part-time job will be strictly limited until you reach full retirement age. Therefore, you should only take your benefit early if you cannot live without it or if you have a terminal illness. Keep in mind, however, that because you are getting a lower benefit, your spouse will get a lower survivor's benefit.

For many people, waiting until age seventy is a good decision because you would receive a significantly greater monthly payment than accepting payments at an earlier age. If you do not need the money for living expenses, it is wise to delay accepting Social Security payments.

Be aware, though, that if you are receiving Medicare benefits, your premiums could go up significantly, especially if you are a high wage earner. For Social Security recipients, there is a provision called "hold harmless" that protects against the effect of higher premiums. This has been put in place to keep the amount of pay received from the government from decreasing in case Medicare premiums increase. If you postpone receiving your Social Security benefit until age seventy, however, that provision does not apply.

Social Security has several other components, including disability benefits for people who can't work and survivor benefits for spouses caring for children. Many people are unaware that when a worker passes away, the system will pay benefits to support the surviving spouse and children. One of my clients died in an accident after he was discharged from the military. His wife had not worked outside the home for a number of years, but with the survivor's benefit and some life insurance, she could stay at home and continue raising her children until they went to college.

When both the husband and wife are still alive, the spouse with the lower income has a choice at retirement age to do either of the following, whichever produces a higher payout:

1. Claim a benefit based on his or her own earnings record, if any.

2. Claim half the benefit that the higher-earning spouse would receive at full retirement age.

If the higher earner were to die, the surviving spouse would usually get an amount equal to the deceased spouse's full retirement benefit. That widow's benefit, as it is often called, can start at age sixty. Let's say John Smith has a benefit of $2,000 a month, and his wife Jane is claiming half that much as her spousal benefit. Together, that totals $3,000. If John were to die, however, Jane would get his benefit of $2,000 but would no longer get the additional $1,000.

If you are divorced and have not remarried, you can choose to claim your benefit based on the earnings record of your ex-spouse (who doesn't have to know you're doing it). You must have been married at least ten years. At your full retirement age, you can get half the amount that your ex-spouse gets, even if your ex-spouse has remarried. It would only make sense to do so, of course, if that amount is greater than what you would get based on your own earnings record.

Social Security is a lot more complicated than it seems at first. I highly recommend you seek qualified advice before claiming your benefits.

Annuities

Another financial vehicle that's a source of guaranteed income is an annuity you can purchase from an insurance company. Let me put it bluntly: *of all the egregious, deceptive, and manipulative things I have observed in the financial industry, annuities seem to be involved in a large percentage of them.* Beware! A lot of unscrupulous people make all sorts of promises when selling annuities. You must know what you are getting into.

An annuity is an insurance product. In essence, you hand over a sum of money (perhaps your life savings) to an insurance company, and it guarantees you regular payments, annual or monthly, for a certain time (perhaps the rest of your life). Annuities can be structured in various ways. Let's look at three basic kinds.

FIXED ANNUITIES

The fixed annuity is, generally, considered the simplest, safest, most straightforward type of annuity. It is relatively easy to understand. You give the insurer a lump sum and in return get a guaranteed payment for a designated period. A fixed annuity can be immediate, meaning those regular payments start as soon as you buy the annuity. Or it can be a deferred plan in which, for example, you pay the insurer when you are fifty, but you do not get payments until age seventy.

Let's say you pay a million dollars and the insurance company, based on current interest rates, agrees to give you $30,000 a year for the rest of your life. However, if you die the next day, the insurance company keeps your million. Or you could structure the deal so that the payouts continue for the rest of your spouse's life, too, and even offer a minimum payout or refund to your heirs. In the end, though, the insurance company gets whatever is left.

Warren Buffett's company, Berkshire Hathaway, sells fixed annuities, so it gives you one benchmark when you talk with agents about purchasing an annuity. Vanguard also has a good low-cost fixed annuity product as does Charles Schwab. Don't hesitate to compare them.

> **An immediate fixed annuity is the only type I would recommend and only under specific, limited circumstances in which income was the paramount concern.**

Always tread carefully with any kind of annuity. Before buying, get an independent opinion and not from the person selling the annuity. An immediate fixed annuity is the only type I would recommend and only under specific, limited circumstances in which income was the paramount concern. Kept simple without a lot of complex riders and features in certain cases, a fixed annuity can serve a useful purpose.

VARIABLE ANNUITIES

When you buy a variable annuity, the insurer puts your money into an account invested in stocks, bonds, and other instruments, minus fees and charges. You can usually choose the investments based on your risk tolerance. As a rule, some portion is guaranteed, although not always.

Be aware that you could lose some of your money. Generally, for an additional fee, you can get a guarantee, either for a minimum balance or an income at some point in your life. However, that amount will depend on market fluctuations, and you will not know up front what it will be.

These products can be so complicated with so many disclosures, hidden fees, and provisions that the paperwork is about the length of *War and Peace*. The world of variable annuities is constantly changing as insurance companies come up with innovative, though not necessarily better, ways to package their wares. I do not recommend investing in variable annuities.

EQUITY-INDEXED ANNUITIES

The third main type is called the equity-indexed annuity. Here, the insurer offers a guaranteed minimum return, plus a variable rate based on the return of a specific stock index. For example, you may be guaranteed a 4 percent return, plus 80 percent of the market return, as measured by the index.

That guarantee can seem appealing, but you can replicate it on your own. The insurance companies that offer these annuities are not the guardians of some magical secret. They are making the same investments that are available to you: stocks, bonds, and real estate.

	IMMEDIATE	FIXED
FUNDING OPTIONS (ACCUMULATION PHASE)	Flexible Premium	Single or Flexible Premium
PAYOUT OPTIONS (DISTRIBUTION PHASE)	Payments begin within one year after funding and are based on Period Certain or Lifetime Provisions.	Payout is deferred. Cash withdrawals allowed after surrender period without penalty or during policy period subject to penalty free withdrawal provisions.
RISK OF PRINCIPAL LOSS	Payments are guaranteed never to decrease. Guarantees are backed by the claims paying ability of the insurance company.	Principle and gains are guaranteed against loss. Guarantees are backed by the claims paying ability of the insurance company.
RATE OF RETURN	Subject to mortality calculations and interest rates at time of issue.	Based on declared and/or guaranteed interest rates.
POSSIBLE FEES	None	Optional income rider or death benefit enhancement fees. Surrender Fees (only apply if money withdrawn in excess of penalty free amount).
LIQUIDITY	None	Return of Premium, Long-Term Care/Home Health Care, Terminal Illness and typically up to 10% of account value per year within surrender fee period.

INDEXED	VARIABLE
Single or Flexible Premium	Single Premium
Payout is deferred. Cash withdrawals allowed after surrender period without penalty or during policy period subject to penalty free withdrawal provisions.	Payout is deferred. Cash withdrawals allowed after surrender period (if applicable) without penalty or during policy period subject to penalty free withdrawal provisions.
Payout is deferred. Cash withdrawals allowed after surrender period without penalty or during policy period subject to penalty free withdrawal provisions.	Payout is deferred. Cash withdrawals allowed after surrender period (if applicable) without penalty or during policy period subject to penalty free withdrawal provisions.
Based on interest credits determined by indexing strategy and/or guaranteed or declared interest rates in fixed accounts.	Based on market performance of subaccounts less any fees.
Optional income rider or death benefit enhancement fees. Surrender Fees (only apply if money withdrawn in excess of penalty free amount).	Transaction Fee (Class A), Surrender Fees (Only apply if money withdrawn in excess of penalty free amount), Policy Fee or Maintenance Fee, Mortality and Expense Fee, Fund Fees (including 12b-1 fees, Management fees, and fund transfer fees). Optional income rider or death benefit enhancement fees.
Return of Premium, Long-Term Care/Home Health Care, Terminal Illness and typically up to 10% of account value per year within surrender fee period.	Return of Premium, Long-Term Care/Home Health Care, Terminal Illness and typically up to 10% of account value per year within surrender fee period.

SUMMARY

Such insurance products can be useful if you are concerned about outliving your money or if you want some sort of risk-sharing arrangement, but always be careful that you're not walking into a minefield.

Be sure you and your advisor talk about the tax consequences of income derived from annuities and the costs associated with them. Companies such as Schwab and Vanguard do offer low- or no-commission and low-fee annuities that can be worth investigating. Just beware that the money in an annuity is no longer yours; you're entitled to receive a regular income stream but there's no guarantee any will be left for heirs. Also, beware that the taxation of annuities can be confusing and create adverse unintended consequences. Get advice from an expert about the wisdom of buying annuities.

Decisions of a Lifetime

As a rule, you cannot change your mind once you have made a choice to accept guaranteed income. Your decision is likely to be irreversible, whether it's choosing the form of your pension, retiring early, or buying an annuity.

You don't get a do-over. If you take the lump-sum option for your pension, you can't go back to the monthly payments. If you retire at sixty-two, you can't undo the reduction of your benefit. If you buy an annuity for a million dollars, you won't get your money back if you change your mind in five years—at least, not without hefty surrender charges. These are serious decisions that can affect the well-being of you and your family for the rest of your days and into the next generation.

PART FOUR

. . .

PITFALLS ALONG YOUR PATH

On your path to financial independence, be prepared to face the threats that could slow you down or stop you in your tracks. Namely, you need strategies for managing taxes, insuring against a variety of risks, and preventing others from derailing your plans.

CHAPTER 11

NOTHING IS CERTAIN
EXCEPT DEATH AND . . .

Taxation is a major obstacle to financial independence. By properly structuring your affairs, you can reduce the tax bite and even eliminate it in retirement. That's possible if you plan for the long term. If you wait until your return is coming due each spring, it will be too late.

C arson had worked forty years for a major company, saving diligently for retirement. He took advantage of a deferred compensation program, and when his employer also began offering a 401(k) plan in the early 1980s, he jumped at the additional opportunity for an immediate savings on his income taxes.

He was in his fifties when he and his wife, Rita, came to my office. They felt confident their retirement account was large enough to see them through their retirement years into old age. They wanted to know whether they should be doing anything specific to get ready.

Yes, plenty, I told them. I congratulated them on giving themselves a jump start on the planning. With a combination of strategies, they would be able to save a bundle on taxes.

Over the decades, as he contributed part of each paycheck to his 401(k), Carson had been able to grow his account impressively without losing any of it to taxes. The IRS staked no claim on his contributions, or on the company's match, or on the investment gains. Uncle Sam would still want his cut but was willing to wait until Carson began withdrawing his money at some point during retirement. That's when he would presumably be in a lower tax bracket. He could begin those withdrawals without a 10 percent penalty as early as age 59½, or he could wait as late as age 70½ when annual withdrawals would become mandatory.

The tax deferral had worked well for the couple during Carson's years with the company. At his income level, Carson would have been in the 40 to 50 percent marginal tax bracket. That meant for every dollar he put into his 401(k), he saved 40 or 50 cents.

Carson decided to retire soon after he and Rita met with me. Consequently, his income level did indeed drop. He was not yet eligible for Social Security benefits and without those paychecks from the company, his tax bracket went down to 15 percent, the next-to-lowest level at the time. The couple needed money to live on, so he was set to begin his 401(k) withdrawals as soon as he was 59½. He figured the 15 percent rate would be a deal compared with what he saved through the years.

It wasn't that simple, though. As we projected his income into the years ahead, we saw that at age seventy, he would be back up to about the 30 percent tax bracket. After all, he and Rita both would be collecting Social Security benefits by then, and his withdrawals from the 401(k) would be mandatory and at a progressively larger percentage each year. With his pension and other investment income, he faced paying nearly as much tax as during his working years.

That's typical for people who have been high wage earners and have a lot of retirement money. A husband and wife who both had good jobs can easily draw about $40,000 each from Social Security, and they would be forced to make annual 401(k) withdrawals starting at age seventy. If they have a $2 million portfolio, those withdrawals will exceed $70,000. Already that adds up to a retirement income of over $150,000. Social Security benefits have become taxable (at their income level, 85 percent of the benefit is taxable), and every dollar withdrawn from a 401(k) is taxable, too. Some clients have proudly shown me their million-dollar 401(k) account. Unfortunately, I have to explain to them that a big chunk of that money is not theirs.

HOW MUCH DO I NEED TO WITHDRAW?

REQUIRED DISTRIBUTIONS FROM A RETIREMENT ACCOUNT AT AGE 70.5

RETIREMENT ACCOUNT VALUE	FIRST YEAR WITHDRAWAL AMOUNT
$ 250,000.00	$ 9,124.00
$ 500,000.00	$ 18,248.18
$ 750,000.00	$ 27,372.26
$ 1,000,000.00	$ 36,496.35
$ 1,500,000.00	$ 54,744.53
$ 2,000,000.00	$ 72,992.70
$ 2,500,000.00	$ 91,240.88
$ 3,000,000.00	$ 109,489.05
$ 5,000,000.00	$ 182,481.75

Note: withdrawal amount changes from year to year and is designed to deplete the account entirely by the end of your life expectancy.

The solution for Carson and Rita was to save on taxes by converting some of those 401(k) assets into a Roth IRA. Each year, while their tax bracket was low, they withdrew as much money as possible without slipping into a higher bracket. After paying the tax on those withdrawals, they then put the money into a Roth IRA account. A Roth has no tax deduction, but none of the money in the account is ever taxed again, even when it's withdrawn, and there is no mandate to do so. By the time Carson reached seventy, we had converted a large portion of his 401(k) into a tax-free Roth. That was possible because we planned ahead and had a decade to do it.

It's not fun to pay the tax up front for a conversion, but for Carson and Rita, the strategy certainly would pay off over time. No matter how much they decided to withdraw from the Roth in the future, that income would not push them into a higher bracket. No longer were they looking at a tax trap. They had planned their way around it by, basically, prepaying the tax at a much lower rate.

A Roth IRA is a valuable strategy for young people's portfolios as well, because it helps manage taxes efficiently for retirement. In recent years, some employers have been offering a Roth 401(k) option as part of their defined contribution plans.

As another part of their tax strategy, Carson and Rita also engaged in a type of income shifting during their retirement. They moved their residence, which made a big difference in their tax picture. They took up residence in Georgia, which exempts a significant portion of all retirees' income. For those over a certain age, the first $65,000 of income is tax-free. That covered the dividends and interest in capital gains from their regular investment account as well as their income from Social Security.

Thanks to this combination of strategies, when in their seventies, this couple was enjoying a seven-figure portfolio but were paying virtually no yearly federal or state income tax.

Lifelong Tax Planning

If you ask people what they expect will be the biggest expense of their lifetime, many will say "Buying a house." But the accurate response for most people would be "Paying my taxes."

Let's say that Jim and Janet Jones work full-time and together earn $175,000 in wages. They have two kids, a mortgage, real estate taxes, and a few charitable deductions. Under the new tax provisions that took effect in 2018, they likely will be in the 22 percent federal bracket and pay about $24,000 in federal income tax. According to studies, the median state tax burden, which includes income tax, property tax, sales tax, and fees, is about 10 percent of income.[4] That's $17,500 more in taxes for the Joneses. Don't forget the Social Security and Medicare tax that was withheld from their pay, which is another $10,000. Altogether, Jim and Janet are paying over $50,000 a year in taxes. If they work for forty years, that's about $2 million paid in taxes, which doesn't even include the inevitable increases due to inflation.

---

4   John S. Kiernan, "2018 Tax Rates by State," WalletHub, May 13, 2018, https://wallethub.com/edu/best-worst-states-to-be-a-taxpayer/2416/.

WHERE DO YOUR TAX DOLLARS GO?

US FEDERAL GOVERNMENT SPENDING BY CATEGORY—2016 BUDGET

SOCIAL SECURITY	Social Security, Retirement, death, and disability benefits.	25%	$825,000,000,000.00
MAJOR HEALTH ENTITLEMENTS	Medicare, Medicaid, Obamacare.	28%	$924,000,000,000.00
INCOME SECURITY	Veterans' benefits, unemployment compensation, food and housing assistance, federal employee retirement, and disability.	18%	$594,000,000,000.00
DEFENSE	Department of Defense funding.	16%	$528,000,000,000.00
INTEREST	Interest on debt issue by the federal government.	6%	$198,000,000,000.00
OTHER	All other budget line items.	7%	$231,000,000,000.00
		100%	$3,300,000,000,000.00

source: https://www.heritage.org/taxes/commentary/where-do-your-tax-dollars-go

According to the Office of Information and Regulatory Affairs, Americans spent more than 8.9 billion hours complying with IRS filing requirements in 2016. That's the equivalent of 4.3 million full-time workers doing nothing but tax return paperwork all year. This costs the economy about $409 billion in lost productivity, the office estimates, which is more than the gross domestic product of thirty-six of the fifty states.[5] Through long-term planning, you can significantly reduce your tax burden. I work with a fair number of retired clients with six-figure incomes who pay virtually no tax. With the new Tax Cut and Jobs Act (TCJA) of 2017, a business owner should not pay more than a mid-20 percent federal tax rate in 2018. There is nothing shifty or illegal about paying a zero or low tax rate. The IRS and state codes provide ample opportunities to reduce taxes. However, it's up to individuals to take advantage of those provisions. My clients simply employ strategies such as the ones that helped Carson and Rita.

> **Americans spent more than 8.9 billion hours complying with IRS filing requirements in 2016. That's the equivalent of 4.3 million full-time workers doing nothing but tax return paperwork all year.**

Most people think of tax planning as something they do once a year when their returns are coming due, but there is not a lot you can do in the weeks before it's time to file. By then, what you owe

---

5   Scott A. Hodge, "The Compliance Costs of IRS Regulations," Tax Foundation, June 15, 2016, https://taxfoundation.org/compliance-costs-irs-regulations.

is what you owe with few exceptions. March is not the time for tax planning—nor is December. Sure, you can list your write-offs for the year, but that's called organizing, not planning. You cannot change what has happened.

Instead, I advocate "structural tax planning"—that is, structuring your life and your affairs through the years to minimize your tax burden overall. True tax planning includes deciding where to live and how you will earn your income. Do you want to live in the Silicon Valley of California, or do you want to live in Texas, which has no state income tax? Will you work for a company and file a W-2 form to report your wages, or will you file a 1099 form as a self-employed contractor? In what will you invest and how? Will you save your money in a regular taxable account, in a tax-free Roth IRA, or in your employer's tax-deferred 401(k) plan?

How you answer any of those questions will have far more impact than what you can write off this year.

Many people know what they *should* do but somehow don't do it. Instead of planning, they react. They look for individual investments that will give them a return sufficient to overcome the tax obligation. However, higher returns generally entail higher risk.

> **The better strategy is not to try to cover a big tax bill, but rather to keep the tax bill at a minimum.**

Investments with a lot of bang can blow up in your face. The better strategy is not to try to cover a big tax bill, but rather to keep the tax bill at a minimum. Taxation amounts to an expense, and how you invest will have a lot to do with how much you owe in taxes—and when.

Tax-Reducing Strategies

Three principal strategies can go far toward minimizing taxes—and not just federal, state, and local income taxes. We also look for ways to reduce taxation on Social Security benefits and Medicare, for example.

The first strategy is timing. You can often save by controlling when you declare your taxable income and deductions. Depending on your situation, you may need a strategy to either defer that income until later tax years, or you may decide it's best to pay the income tax up front to avoid a higher rate later.

The second strategy is income shifting. For Carson and Rita, we saw how they shifted their income to a different state that was more tax-favorable to them. You may be able to save significantly if you can pay your tax in a different jurisdiction. You might find ways to shift income to other members in your family who may pay tax at a lower rate, or to shift income to an entity such as your business. Determine what would be in your best interest.

The third strategy is to convert income so you are deriving it from an activity that is taxed at a lower rate. The wages from a job, for example, tend to be taxed heavily. They are subject not only to income tax but also to taxes for Social Security and Medicare benefits. If you can take your income as capital gains, the rate will be lower. In fact, it could be zero.

Let's look at several types of federal taxes of varying rates: ordinary income tax, qualified dividends, long-term capital gains, self-employment, FICA taxes, and the AMT (alternative minimum tax). In addition, each state has its own set of rules. Some states, such as Florida, South Dakota, Texas, and Washington, don't have any state income taxes. Others, such as California, have a top rate exceeding 13 percent.

TYPES OF INCOME TAX
Ordinary income tax
Qualified dividends
Long-term capital gains
Self-employment and FICA taxes
Alternative minimum tax

ORDINARY INCOME TAX

You pay ordinary income tax on the money you make at your job: wages, salaries, tips, commissions, and bonuses. It is also the rate you pay on interest from a savings account, a bond, or on certain types of dividends. You pay it on rent you collect. Sole proprietorships, partnerships, LLCs, or flow-through business entities also generate ordinary income. In 2018 the top marginal tax rate was 37 percent on income exceeding $500,000 for individuals and $600,000 for married couples filing jointly. (On top of that, since 2013, the Affordable Care Act has added a 0.9 percent Medicare surtax on income over $200,000 for individuals and $250,000 for married couples filing jointly.) The bottom bracket was at 10 percent for income up to $9,525 for individuals and $19,050 for married couples filing jointly.

There is now a new category of ordinary income, thanks to the Tax Cut and Jobs Act of 2017 (TCJA). It's called qualified business income. Starting in 2018, an individual taxpayer may be able to deduct 20 percent of qualified business income from a partnership, S corporation, or sole proprietorship as well as 20 percent of aggregate qualified REIT dividends and qualified publicly traded partnership income. While it is beyond the scope of this book to delve into the nuances of the law, suffice it to say that, for many business owners, the marginal tax rate on ordinary income will be reduced by 20 percent.

QUALIFIED DIVIDENDS AND LONG-TERM CAPITAL GAINS

The tax rate is considerably lower, potentially zero, on money you make as qualified dividends you receive from your investments, and from the long-term capital gains you make from the sale of investments or property you have held for more than a year. The rate for both is the same, at one of three levels: 0, 15 percent, and 20 percent. (In addition, the Affordable Care Act levies a 3.8 percent tax on net investment income for individuals with income over $200,000, or $250,000 for couples.)

The 2018 rate on qualified dividends and long-term capital gains was zero for single taxpayers with an income up to $38,600, or up to $77,200 for couples. The rate was 15 percent for single taxpayers with an income up to $425,800, or up to $479,000 for couples filing jointly. For higher incomes, the rate was 20 percent.

Consider the difference: If you are in the top bracket and make a dollar as ordinary income, you pay 37 cents of it in tax. But if you make a dollar as a capital gain and you and your spouse together earn less than $77,200, you pay no tax on it.

SELF-EMPLOYMENT AND FICA TAXES

Independent contractors are subject to a self-employment tax that covers the Federal Insurance Contributions Act (FICA) levies for Social Security and Medicare. Employees who work for a company pay FICA taxes, too, but only half as much. The employer pays an equal share. If you are your own employer, you get to pay both shares, but at least you can deduct half that tax as an adjustment to income, somewhat reducing the burden.

For 2018, the self-employment tax was 15.3 percent on the first $128,400 of net income. That percentage includes 12.4 percent in Social Security tax and 2.9 percent in Medicare tax. For higher incomes, the 2.9 percent tax continues but not the Social Security tax. Individuals making over $200,000 and couples making over $250,000 also pay the 0.9 percent Medicare surtax. That percentage is the same whether you are an employee or self-employed.

THE ALTERNATIVE MINIMUM TAX

The US Congress has created two tax codes: the standard one and the AMT, which limits deductions. The AMT was established in 1969 to ensure that the wealthiest citizens could not escape their federal obligation through overuse of tax breaks. You must pay the AMT if a calculation shows it to be higher than the regular rate. The complexities are beyond the scope of this book, but be aware: *taxpayers who think they have structured their affairs to minimize their tax under the regular code are often surprised to discover they owe more.* The TCJA significantly reduced the number of people who will be subject to AMT in tax years beginning in 2018. Remember, though, that most of the provisions of the TCJA are set to expire after 2025.

Investments and Taxation

A variety of techniques can be used to manage taxes when investing in publicly traded securities through brokerage or retirement accounts, including location optimization and tax diversification.

Location optimization simply means choosing investments that will keep taxes at a minimum and position them into the proper accounts. The central question is this: Where are you putting your investments—into a fully taxable account or a retirement account that is either tax free or tax deferred?

For an account in which you pay taxes annually on the income, choose tax-efficient investments such as index funds, ETFs, municipal bonds, stocks or mutual funds that pay qualified dividends, or stocks that you expect to hold for more than a year.

By contrast, the tax-sheltered nature of a retirement account makes it more suitable to investments in actively managed funds and trading strategies. Actively managed funds are not recommended for the reasons stated in Chapter 6, but if you do invest that way, at least do it in a retirement account so you have a better chance of getting a decent return. If you are investing in REITs, place those in your retirement accounts, along with high-yield bonds that are taxed at the ordinary income rate.

Tax diversification is the practice of dividing your investments among accounts that offer a variety of tax options. The three principal accounts are (1) a regular brokerage account on which you pay tax each year, (2) a tax-deferred retirement account such as a 401(k) or an IRA, and (3) a tax-free Roth account. Ideally, you should invest in all three types. Many people are proud of their sizable 401(k), but that's all they have. In retirement, they will have no choice but to withdraw from it—and every dollar will be taxable, perhaps at an even higher rate than during their working years. If they had a Roth account as well and a regular brokerage account, they would not need to lean so heavily on the 401(k).

When you have tax diversity, you have choices. I have met many people with a tax burden that they might have avoided if they had seen it coming. They expected one thing, and another thing happened. Such is life, and such are taxes. The rules can change.

Playing to Win

There is no one-size-fits-all approach to tax planning. If you are charitably inclined, you can take one path; if you want to leave most of your money to your heirs, you can take another. If you own a small business, you can write off expenses in creative ways, such as deducting part of the cost of your car if you use it for business, or the cost of a week in Hawaii if most of the trip was for a conference.

Whatever your situation, tax planning is for the long term. Think about tomorrow, not just today. It might seem appropriate to defer taxes so you pay less this year, for example, but would you do that if you knew the consequence would be paying more in later years? Keep in mind that the rules can change over the years, rendering once-smart strategies obsolete or ineffective. The TCJA changed the rules in some deeply embedded tax strategies. While the techniques and tactics have to adapt, the principles of tax planning are timeless.

Different types of income are taxed differently. As part of your long-term vision, consider the character and timing of your income.

As we have seen, that's all part of the strategy for converting your human capital—the wage-earning potential of your early years—into the type of assets that will grow most efficiently to secure your financial independence.

Overall, the best long-term strategy is to prepare for a number of potential tax environments while taking advantage of opportunities to defer or shift income to your advantage. Consider the tax ramifications of everything you do and play to win.

CHAPTER 12

INSURING AGAINST RISK

Insurance is fundamental to financial well-being. At every turn are threats to the quest for prosperity. Death, accidents, and illnesses have left many families in turmoil. Insurance, in its various forms, is the means to manage those risks.

My old friend Tom had a great laugh and an adventurous spirit that made folks want to be around him. When he walked into my office not long after the 9/11 attacks, I recognized him right away, and the memories came flooding back. I hadn't seen him in years.

After we chatted awhile, Tom said, "I've decided to enlist in the National Guard, and I want to go through the Special Forces course. He knew I had been a US Army Ranger and had passed the Special Forces Assessment and Selection Course. "David, I was wondering if you could give me some tips on what I need to do to make it in."

I studied his face for a moment and saw he was earnest. "Tom, why would you consider that?" I asked him. "I mean, that's something for young guys to do." He was in his mid-30s now and not exactly in tip-top shape to pass the selection. Besides, he had a family to support. Was he planning to quit his job? He was doing quite well in a sales position, a good match for his outgoing personality.

"This is just something I've got to do," he told me, and I nodded. I understood the feeling.

I didn't see Tom again until about a year after that when he came to my office again. He told me that his plan to join the Special Forces hadn't worked out.

"I broke my foot on the first day out there," he explained, "so that was that. At least I got my job back." I couldn't help but think he had been fortunate on both counts.

"David, this time I'm here to hire you," he told me. "It's time I got a financial advisor to help get my stuff in order." And so we worked together to set up his investment accounts to serve him and his family well. We reviewed his will and other documents, as well as his beneficiary designations. He asked me to check out his life insurance policies—he had three, dating back several years—to make sure they were in good standing and sufficient for his family's needs.

A month later, I got a call from a mutual friend. "Have you seen Tom?" he asked. Nobody had seen or heard from him in days. I called his wife Susie. She was deeply worried.

Soon after, another friend found Tom's body. He had taken his own life.

Tom had been planning his exit all along, and I couldn't see it. He had been working diligently to ensure everything was in place so his wife and two kids would have a good future—but not one that included him.

I learned that Tom had been under treatment for bipolar disorder. Susie later won a settlement in a lawsuit she filed over the pharmaceutical cocktail that had worsened his condition instead of helping him.

Susie would be all right—financially, at least. Her husband's life insurance had been in effect long enough not to exclude suicide, and she put the settlement money from the lawsuit into a trust for their children's schooling and other needs. She and the kids also received Social Security survivor benefits, so she was able to continue devoting herself full time to raising them. She returned to work only after they were older, beginning a career working with veterans who were struggling with various personal issues.

Tom's family would be alright financially. We had made sure of that.

Solutions to the Pitfalls

You never really know. Uncertainty swirls around us, and that is why we must plan for the worst even as we pursue the best. Tom's version of planning was tragic, but even in his fog of drugs and mental turmoil, he provided for his family. He wanted the best for his loved ones, and that is why he came to see me. He didn't recognize the pain he would be inflicting.

In its various forms, insurance is a solution to many of the pitfalls you could face along the path to financial independence.

I often recommend life insurance to my clients as well as disability insurance. The death, injury, or illness of the breadwinner can devastate a family financially as well as emotionally. Though it is hard to acknowledge that prospect, we must. By anticipating what could happen, we can prepare for any contingency.

Insuring against death and disability is, in effect, insuring against the loss of earning power. In its various forms, insurance is a solution to many of the pitfalls you could face along the path to financial independence. By purchasing insurance, you reduce the financial blow of major risks that could befall you. In this chapter, we will review the kinds of insurance products you should consider.

COMMON TYPES OF INSURANCE
Life
Disability
Health
Longevity
Liability
Specialty
Business

LIFE INSURANCE

When you are younger and in the accumulation stage of life, you need life insurance if the loss of your wages would put your family in financial trouble. As you get older and accumulate more assets, the need for protection goes down, which is why I generally recommend term coverage. It is one of two main categories of life insurance; the other is whole-life or permanent insurance.

With term insurance, you pay a premium for a policy covering a specific period, say ten, twenty, or thirty years. At the end of that term, you stop paying, and your coverage stops too. A permanent policy, by contrast, is not limited to a term and generates cash value through the years. If funds are not borrowed from the policy while you are alive, when you die, the cash value and death benefit can pass to your heirs.

Permanent insurance can play a key role in estate planning, which we will discuss in Chapter 15. However, it is a lot more expensive than term insurance and usually carries high commissions. Be careful. This is where we observe many of the abuses in the insurance industry. As a rule, you will be better off getting more term insurance instead of investing in a smaller permanent policy.

The technique of laddering works well with term insurance policies. For example, young people may buy ten-year, twenty-year, and thirty-year policies so the shorter ones phase out as they gradually build the savings and investments that make the insurance less necessary. That is a great way to minimize premiums while covering a much larger need in the early years.

In addition, as mentioned previously, the Social Security system provides a type of life insurance in the form of survivor benefits paid to the surviving spouse if that spouse is raising children, and to the children themselves until they are eighteen years old. When calculating how much life insurance you need, you should take that benefit into account as well.

DISABILITY INSURANCE

The likelihood of becoming incapacitated is greater than the likelihood of dying young, so disability insurance should be included in your risk management. In Chapter 5, we looked at this coverage as an element of employee benefits; however, you may need to purchase more of it depending on how much money you and your family need to get by. If you were bedridden and unable to work for a month, or six months, or a year, what expenses would you need to cover? It's a straightforward calculation.

Short-term disability insurance covers a temporary need—for example, if you break your leg while skiing and are laid up a few weeks. Many employers provide short-term policies. Some states, such as California, automatically enroll employees in a state disability plan. Such programs are funded through minimal payroll deductions.

Long-term disability insurance protects against debilitating injuries. If you are a surgeon, for example, and lose a hand in an auto accident, this type of insurance will protect you against long-term loss of income. Most large companies will provide long-term coverage, usually at about two-thirds of the employee's base pay. An additional commercial policy may be needed to fully replace the loss of income. Take into consideration that Social Security provides a benefit for permanent disability, but it isn't much and it's hard to get.

HEALTH INSURANCE

Without coverage for medical care, a serious injury or illness would quickly wipe out most people financially. Originally, health insurance was conceived as protection against catastrophic illness. It has morphed into coverage for routine procedures as well, which have become increasingly expensive.

You can get traditional health insurance from your employer or purchase an individual policy.

An alternative to traditional health insurance is membership in a health care-sharing ministry, most of which are Christian based. This option is exploding in popularity and can be affordable for people who lack coverage by an employer. Most of these organizations, however, limit the dollar amount of expenses they will cover, and unlike traditional insurers, they are not prohibited from turning away people with pre-existing conditions. Go to www.healthcaresharing. org for information about the Alliance of Health Care Sharing Ministries (AHCSM).

> **Originally, health insurance was conceived as protection against catastrophic illness. It has morphed into coverage for routine procedures as well, which have become increasingly expensive.**

Another option is buying a temporary health care plan, which used to be for only ninety days but can be extended to up to thirty-six months. United Health Care, for example, has a short-term option for catastrophic coverage, but it won't cover pre-existing conditions. Go to https://www.uhc.com/individual-and-family/short-term-health-insurance for details.

If you have the choice, opt for a plan that allows contributions to a health savings account (HSA). If your plan meets certain coverage and deductible requirements, you are eligible to contribute between $3,450 and $7,900 to a savings-type account. The amount depends on whether you are single or included in a family plan, and whether you are under or over the age of fifty-five.

This annual contribution is a deduction from your income for tax purposes and the money can be withdrawn tax-free at any time to pay for medical expenses. If possible, the best strategy is to let the money accumulate, invest it in stocks, and let it grow tax-free. Later in life, you can withdraw the funds tax-free for medical expenses incurred anytime since the date you established the HSA. In effect, it is a turbo-charged Roth IRA. Not only can the money be withdrawn tax-free, but you also get a tax deduction for the contribution. If you make it to age sixty-five with funds left over, you can take them out penalty-free for any reason and only pay tax on the earnings. As with all tax breaks, there are a number of rules to follow, but this can be quite a lucrative strategy.

LONGEVITY INSURANCE

> **If you have the choice, opt for a plan that allows contributions to a health savings account (HSA).**

Health insurance will pay for medical care at a nursing home but not for residency there. Nor will it pay for extended home health care. Likewise, Medicare does not pay for long-term facility costs. For that reason, the insurance industry devised long-term-care coverage, which I like to call longevity insurance. Generally, it will pay for the costs of staying in a facility for a specific time. Or it will pay for the cost of home care for people who need assistance with basic activities of daily living, such as eating, bathing, dressing, or going to the bathroom.

However, most of the insurers that originally offered such coverage exited the market because they drastically underestimated the costs involved. Those that still provide long-term-care insurance offer policies that are somewhat limited and often expensive. Most limit coverage to three, four, or perhaps five years and put a cap on the amount they pay.

Long-term-care policies can be useful in some circumstances, but the people who need them most are often the ones who cannot afford them. And those who can afford those policies do not need them because they have done a good job of accumulating financial assets. They can self-insure.

LIABILITY INSURANCE

Most people will acquire some form of property and casualty insurance to protect themselves against risks that, even if unlikely, could devastate them. Often, the insurance is

> **Long-term-care policies can be useful in some circumstances, but the people who need them most are often the ones who cannot afford them.**

required, such as to obtain a mortgage or drive a car. The amount of insurance should be sufficient to replace the home or car if necessary, but it is pointless to carry more coverage than the property is worth.

It's a good practice to periodically estimate the cost to rebuild your home and make sure you have sufficient coverage. Your coverages can fall behind if they aren't automatically adjusted upward for the effect of inflation. On the other hand, if you own an old car that's not worth much, consider dropping the auto insurance. Of course, you need to retain the liability portion, but the collision part, as it's called, is optional if your car is paid off.

To better protect yourself if you need to file an insurance claim, you should walk around your house with a video camera and record everything you own, including what is inside drawers and cabinets. Some companies will provide that service for you, documenting your possessions for a reasonable fee so you are ready to deal with an insurance adjuster if necessary.

Your homeowners and auto policies will have a liability portion to protect you if you damage someone else's property or if someone claims an injury was your fault. As you build your assets toward financial independence, you can become a target for lawsuits. If you are involved in a serious auto accident, for example, you are much more likely to be sued if you have deep pockets, despite the merits of the case. Be sure to have adequate liability coverage. Set the limit as high as you can on your policies. If you have accumulated substantial financial assets, you will need more coverage than the minimum your state mandates.

I also recommend an umbrella policy, which provides liability coverage in addition to all the other coverages you have. If your auto policy provides $500,000 worth of liability coverage, for example, and you also have a $2 million umbrella policy, you will be covered for up to the limits of both policies. The total liability coverage on your auto, homeowners', and umbrella policies should cover at least your net worth—or a multiple of your net worth to be safe.

SPECIALTY INSURANCE

A variety of other types of specialty insurances are available. For example, in California, you might need earthquake insurance; in North Carolina, flood insurance. Your needs will vary depending on your situation. Be sure to work with an independent agent you trust who will take a holistic view of the risks you face and is not simply out to sell you products.

BUSINESSES INSURANCE

Business owners face a greater number of liability issues, some specific to their industry. If you own a business, your advisor or insurance broker should be intimately familiar with the specific risks associated with what you do. You should at least have liability coverage in case someone slips and falls on your premises. In addition, many professionals get coverage for "errors and omissions" such as a bad recommendation that causes harm. A form of that is malpractice insurance, which most physicians obtain to cover them if patients sue.

Many organizations obtain key-person, or business-continuity, insurance in case the owner or other critical personnel were to die or leave. The pay-out sustains operations and buys time to find highly qualified replacements. Otherwise, the business might fold.

The brevity of this section doesn't imply that business insurance is not a serious issue. Don't short-change your business insurance policies. An advisory team including a financial advisor, attorney, and insurance agent well versed in asset protection is a must for all business owners serious about achieving financial independence.

Don't Overdo It

Insurance brings you peace of mind as you strive to build your fortunes in the face of threats that could imperil your finances. Don't overdo it, though. Many people pay too much for insurances they don't need. Niche insurances such as dismemberment coverage, mortgage life insurance, and cancer insurance are, most of the time, a waste of money. In reviewing policies for clients, I have often found ample opportunity to reduce costs by eliminating unnecessary or duplicate coverage.

Some insurance companies and brokers have bad reputations, earned for good reason. Look for an independent insurance agent, and before you pay that person a visit, figure out your requirements.

> **Many people pay too much for insurances they don't need.**

If you want life insurance, for example, take the time to calculate the extent of your need before going to a broker.

The best advisor, frankly, is likely to be someone who doesn't sell insurance but understands the products and can offer unbiased recommendations. Think of it this way: an insurance policy is something you should buy, not something you should be sold.

CHAPTER 13

HOW YOUR PLAN CAN GET DERAILED

Despite your best intentions, outside influences can severely hamper your efforts to attain financial independence. Those forces are sometimes beyond your control, but you can anticipate what could derail your financial plan and protect yourself.

"I need help with my portfolio," an old acquaintance, Rudy, told me when he stopped by my office one day.

Since we had last talked, Rudy had attained his law degree and started a private practice, later moving to North Carolina, where his wife, June, had a great career opportunity. This couple represented a lot of brainpower and, together, they were earning between $300,000 and $400,000 a year. They had managed to save a significant sum for investments.

They had also managed to lose a significant sum. I looked at their figures. Over the course of just two years, their investments had taken a plunge—in the first year by 25 percent and in the second year by 50 percent. This wasn't in the depths of the Great Recession, but during the boom years of the recovery that followed.

I looked up and nodded. "I've got to agree. You're absolutely right, Rudy. You need help."

Rudy and June's portfolio was the antithesis of what I would recommend. "I'll be happy to help you," I told him, "but just know that your portfolio is going to look completely different from what I see here."

Until they spiraled into this investment mess, Rudy and June were on track for early retirement. They spent a lot, but they were also setting aside enough money to give themselves options other than continuing their labors—that is, had they invested it wisely. Moreover, Rudy was beginning to feel burned out in the legal profession. The two of them wanted to retire by age fifty, and they had big plans to build a multimillion-dollar house. They already had spent $50,000 on architectural work, before even laying the first brick.

Now, after this debacle, neither their retirement nor their fancy house would be possible anytime soon. I recommended they bail out of their construction plans and refocus on their new reality. As they attempted to rebuild their savings, could they still afford a private chef in their home? Could they afford expensive vacations such as the one they took to the Napa Valley where they spent $15,000 for a wine collection?

Where did Rudy and June go wrong? As many people do, they were looking for the next big way to make a lot of money. Rudy had been talking to a lawyer who had set up a little side business investing people's money. That alone should have been a warning sign. The lawyer had put on a good show and made big promises, so this couple, in the aftermath of the financial crisis, handed over all their money, which he invested in individual stocks. His surefire formula backfired. Much of their savings vanished, and they were set back at least ten or fifteen years.

Their guru *du jour* had not put them into a diversified portfolio with the ability to weather a downturn and recover. Instead, he had picked a basket of losers that were never coming back. Their money had disappeared.

Frankly, though, they were more than the victims of an incompetent investment advisor. They also were victims of their own greed. That lawyer sent them down a dreadful path, but Rudy and June willingly followed it. They lost perspective as they entertained their high hopes for a luxurious early retirement and a mansion of their own. I see similar scenarios quite often, though usually on a smaller scale. Eager for a buck, people buy expensive annuities that are inappropriate for their situation or get suckered into investment schemes that bleed them dry.

That's how dreams get derailed. That's how people can jump the tracks, leaving their portfolios and financial plans in the wreckage. They listen to a smooth talker or glib salesperson who claims to possess the secret for success, even though anyone with such sublime insight likely wouldn't share it. As they chase after returns and pursue the latest investment fads, they exhaust themselves—and their portfolios.

Derailed by Wall Street

I'm not out to bash all of Wall Street. I have a lot of friends on the Street who genuinely try to do what's right for their clients. Still, the stock brokerage system (as well as the system that purports to give advice to clients) is flawed and entails significant risks. Brokers who start out with the best intentions occasionally end up in bad places, saying later that one little thing led to another. Bernie Madoff perpetrated one of the largest frauds in US history, but he was not a swindler when he started out on Wall Street. He descended step by step.

Such bad situations can develop because the incentives on Wall Street are not aligned with the investing client. Brokers work under a suitability standard—that is, their recommendations are supposed to be suitable for the client. Sounds good, but sometimes the investment products the brokers deem to be most suitable are those that line their own pockets most lucratively. The broker wins even if the client loses.

IN THE CONSUMERS' INTEREST

By contrast, advisors who function as fiduciaries are required by law to put the client's interests above their own. Working with a fiduciary,

> **Working with a fiduciary, particularly one who charges a flat fee instead of an asset-based fee, eliminates many of the problems that could derail your plans.**

particularly one who charges a flat fee instead of an asset-based fee, eliminates many of the problems that could derail your plans.

In the world of most goods and services, a flat fee is common. Consumers are accustomed to paying a set price based on the value of the product or the complexity of the service. A restaurant doesn't size up your wealth to decide what to charge for your steak dinner. No matter who you are, you are expected to pay the going price for the value you get.

WHAT'S THE DIFFERENCE BETWEEN AN ADVISOR AND A BROKER?

- Under the Investment Advisers Act of 1940, a registered investment advisor (RIA) is required to act as a fiduciary. RIAs must put your interests above their own and declare any conflicts of interest that may arise.

- A broker, or registered representative, is required only to recommend investments that are "suitable" for you. In other words, brokers can legally put their own interests above yours when recommending investments "suitable" for the situation.

When I started in the industry just before the turn of the millennium, the concept of a fee-only fiduciary was novel. Today, even some stockbrokers are co-opting the concept: instead of charging a commission per transaction, they charge a continuing fee based on the amount of the client's assets they manage.

Nonetheless, they still extricate vast sums of money from unsuspecting clients for advice of dubious value. The prevailing attitude among the habitués of Wall Street is this: *Why would we charge a flat fee? That's not the way to make the most money.* That's their truth, but a flat fee is the fairest way to charge. Be careful that you are not dealing with what I call fake fiduciaries. They do not necessarily do what is best for the client.

HOW IS YOUR ADVISOR PAID?
This list outlines your options:

Commission-based	These advisors earn a commission on the financial products they sell to their clients.
Fee-based	These advisors use a fee structure for some services while they earn commissions on other services they provide.
Fee-only	These advisors do not accept any fees or compensation based on product sales. They are compensated solely by their clients. Fee-only advisors have fewer inherent conflicts of interest. They offer their services under several compensation arrangements: • **Assets Under Management (AUM):** Clients are charged a percentage of the assets being managed. • **Hourly:** Some financial planners choose to go with a simpler fee structure of charging by the hour. • **Per Account Fee:** There are firms that charge a single flat fee per managed asset account. Typically, they do not provide planning services. • **Fixed Retainer:** The amount determined at the outset of the engagement is based on the complexity of the client's situation. It changes as the professional relationship is renewed from time to time or in response to changes in the client's needs or use of services, not the size or growth of the client's portfolio

Paying Investment Fees

Other forces that can get your financial plan off track include the variety of fees you pay on investments. Never underestimate the toll that those fees can take on the growth of your portfolio.

To invest with a major firm on Wall Street, according to many estimates, it will cost about 3 percent of your money. Different types of cost will make up this 3 percent and include many of the following: brokerage account fees, trade commissions, mutual fund transaction fees, expense ratios, sales loads, and management or advisory fees.

Let's say you were to start out with $100,000 and could maintain a return of 8 percent over thirty years. You would finish by topping a million dollars—about $1,006,000. However, your 3 percent in fees would reduce your return effectively to 5 percent, so you would end up with only about $432,000. If you could trim just 1 percentage point off your fees to attain an effective rate of 6 percent, you would have about $574,000. If you could manage to net 7 percent, you would come in at about $761,000.

The chart on the next page shows another example of the effects of various levels of asset and management fees.

When you purchase an investment, there are a many fees you should monitor, including the sales commission fees or broker fees. Also know the expense ratio, which reflects how much a mutual fund or ETF pays annually for portfolio management, administration, marketing, and other operating costs. The expense ratio is expressed as a percentage of the fund's average net assets. It can range from rock bottom—a couple hundredths of a percent at institutions such as Schwab and Vanguard—all the way up to 0.5 to 2 percent per year for an actively managed mutual fund in more exotic asset classes. Consider the difference between an expense ratio of 0.02 percent and

2.00 percent. That's two dollars versus two hundred dollars for every $10,000 you invest.

Also, be aware of transaction costs. Previously, buying or selling a stock through a broker would cost $200 or $300 per transaction. Today, with online trading, buying and selling are often free or only cost a few dollars. However, some strategies carry transaction costs you might not pay directly. These are what we call "market impact costs" and "underlying transaction costs." When you buy a car, for example, you're paying more for it than the dealer paid, which is called the "spread." The same concept applies when buying stocks. When you buy through a broker, you're paying more than you would in a direct transaction with the owner of the stocks. These underlying costs affect the returns you'll receive on your investment.

In the 401(k) realm, learn about the administrative and miscellaneous fees that drag down returns. For example, some funds impose redemption fees. Some brokers impose account fees. There are expenses called 12b-1, or trailer fees, that the manager pays to the broker who sells the fund to investors. Such fees apply to all types of investment accounts, depending on the type of advisor, but the 401(k) market can be particularly egregious in charging them.

Keep an eye on all those expenses, as they could significantly diminish your ability to accumulate wealth over time.

A Beating in the Market

The stock market is a great place to build wealth and has served investors well for generations, but trouble comes when investors feel certain they can outsmart the market. That's when it takes an unexpected swing, dashing their hopes. The fault, so often, is not in

PORTFOLIO VALUE FROM INVESTING $100,000 OVER TWENTY YEARS

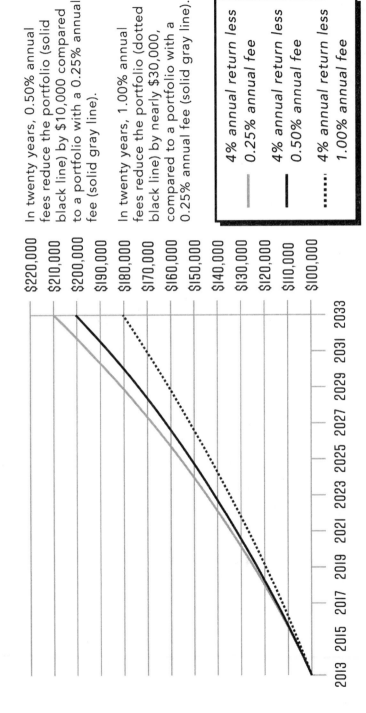

In twenty years, 0.50% annual fees reduce the portfolio (solid black line) by $10,000 compared to a portfolio with a 0.25% annual fee (solid gray line).

In twenty years, 1.00% annual fees reduce the portfolio (dotted black line) by nearly $30,000, compared to a portfolio with a 0.25% annual fee (solid gray line).

4% annual return less 0.25% annual fee

4% annual return less 0.50% annual fee

4% annual return less 1.00% annual fee

the market but in the investors themselves. Because they're chasing returns, they buy when they should sell and vice versa.

Increasingly, investors are wising up to how hard it is to beat the market, a truth discussed in Chapters 6 and 7. Numerous research studies have indicated that actively managed mutual funds do not gain enough in performance to cover their costs. For example, a study of 3,870 mutual funds from 1984 to 2015 found they had lower average returns (after subtracting the percentage for fees) than the Russell 3000 index for the same period. The managed funds, as a whole, returned 9.34 percent while the index returned 10.68 percent.[6]

This study shows managers failed to perform better in the long run than the market index they are trying to top. They do so occasionally but not reliably and consistently over long periods. If professional money managers can't do it, then do-it-yourselfers and part-timers can't, either. *Those who try to beat the market are likely to take a beating in the market.*

MUTUAL FUNDS

Mutual funds want to promote themselves, of course. Those that have a good year or two will proclaim their brilliance. Often, they will show a random time frame in which they look stellar, but they don't shine so brightly if those dates are shifted one way or the other. For example, Fund A could be performing well and Fund B poorly, so Fund B is closed and rolled into Fund A. In that way, the poor track record of Fund B disappears. Fund companies also cherry-pick the timeframe of the records they show publicly. To protect your

---

6   Philipp Meyer-Brauns, "Mutual Fund Performance through a Five-Factor Lens," Dimensional Fund Advisors, 2016.

investments, look for lengthy performance records and watch out for deceptive practices!

The chart on the next page shows performance graphs over time of various funds.

Many investors jump in and out of funds, dramatically influencing individual returns. Dalbar Inc., an independent research firm in Boston, has regularly compared the performance of investor portfolios to the major stock market indices over a twenty-year period. The research has consistently demonstrated how investor behavior influences results. A mutual fund might show a 10 percent return over time, for example, but the investor who is chasing returns might earn only 3 percent.

> **Trouble comes when investors feel certain they can outsmart the market. That's when it takes an unexpected swing, dashing their hopes. The fault, so often, is not in the market but in the investors themselves.**

Human nature often leads investors astray, as you will see in Chapter 14. At cocktail parties, they brag about their winners and don't mention their losers. They praise the so-called prowess of stock pickers who got in early on Apple or Microsoft. They don't mention their own losses from speculating in the tech bubble.

The sad truth is that smart people with great careers often do poorly in the stock market. In school, they got good grades by studying hard and using their brain power, so that's how they try to earn an A in the market. In the realm of publicly traded stocks, however, you can win without much studying. Getting a B requires a lot less effort, and it takes you where you need to go. In striving for an A, many investors end up failing.

Derailed in the Workforce

Your employer, too, can derail your plan, most directly by laying you off, firing you, or going out of business. Losing a job, particularly when you are well into your career, can be devastating. To protect yourself, always stay ahead of the game. Continue to network, develop your skills, and keep your résumé up to date. Don't stop investing in yourself. Even years later, a former employer's misfortunes can become yours. For example, after the bankruptcy dust settled in Detroit and in the California cities of Stockton and San Bernardino, municipal retirees found their health care benefits either slashed or eliminated. One of my clients worked at a Fortune 500 company for the first fifteen or twenty years of his career. He was promised a pension, but the company went bankrupt. After the plan was turned over to the Pension Benefit Guaranty Corporation, he got only about a quarter of what he had expected.

A mutual fund might show a 10 percent return over time, but the investor who is chasing returns might earn only 3 percent.

FEW MUTUAL FUNDS HAVE SURVIVED AND OUTPERFORMED

PERFORMANCE PERIODS ENDING DECEMBER 31, 2017

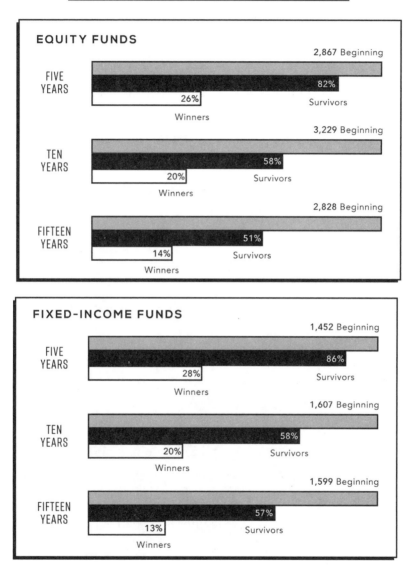

The sample includes funds at the beginning of the five-, ten-, and fifteen-year periods ending December 31, 2017. Survivors are funds that had returns for every month in the sample period. Winners are funds that survived and outperformed their respective Morningstar category index over the period.

Graph Source: Mutual Fund Landscape, Dimensional Fund Advisors, 2018.

Perhaps your employer is shaking up your world by asking you to relocate. If so, be sure that the move would be good for your career and for your family. How is the quality of life in the new location? If the cost of living will be higher, will you get a raise to make up for it? How much will the company pay for your relocation? Selling and buying a house can get expensive, so who will bear that cost? Don't assume that relocation will be positive. You could lose your job after relocating and need to find other opportunities there, so be sure you are moving to a place that would suit you for the long term.

You also can get off track in the workforce by choosing your employment benefits unwisely. Don't assume your employer knows what's right for you and your personal situation. As we saw in Chapter 5, you may need additional disability and life insurance to supplement what you get at work. Be sure you have a health care plan that is appropriate for what you and your family need. And in case you lose your job, consider getting coverage outside the workplace for your life and disability insurance.

Also, your workplace retirement plan may be insufficient to meet your goals. Many 401(k) and related plans have been notorious for offering poor investment selections with high fees. The US Department of Labor, in fact, has fined or penalized about 75 percent of the plans it has audited. Get good advice before participating. If your retirement plan is weak, we sometimes suggest investing in it only to the extent that your employer gives you a matching contribution. Workplace retirement plans are significantly better than a decade ago, but many are still poorly constructed.

Derailed by the Government

One of the early movers in the e-cigarette industry was derailed when new government regulations changed the rules on what types of e-cigarettes and products could be sold online. The retailer's sales plummeted about 75 percent in one month. Such is the power of the government to influence the acquisition of wealth. It happens to businesses, and it happens to individuals.

The government's power to tax—and to change the tax rules—has a profound effect on personal finances, as we saw in Chapter 11. What will happen with future rates? We can only guess. How might the government change the rules for deductions or retirement plans?

If you are basing your retirement goals on a favorable tax rule, understand that the government giveth and taketh away depending on the political climate. That's one reason you need tax diversity in your retirement planning, as we examined earlier: besides a taxable account, I suggest you contribute to a Roth IRA account, for example, as well as to your traditional IRA or 401(k). Though the rules can change, you can keep your options open.

> **Take a close look at the forces at work in the industry you have chosen for your career, assess your prospects for success, and adjust your plan accordingly.**

Regulations imposed on industries can determine the fate of the company where you work, potentially disrupting your career. Environmental legislation has significantly affected jobs in the coal industry, as just one example. Government subsidies can prop up an industry for a while as it makes inroads, but what happens when those subsidies cease? Trade and tariff policies, both domestically and abroad, also can wield a huge influence on how well certain industries can compete. Ask a farmer or a steelworker.

The bottom line is that government policies can have a significant impact on your ability to accumulate wealth. Take a close look at the forces at work in the industry you have chosen for your career, assess your prospects for success, and adjust your plan accordingly.

Move Full Speed Ahead

The forces that can derail a financial plan come in a variety of forms. Some people lose their fortunes to advisors with a crystal ball, and some slip up simply by trying to outwit the market. Sometimes, plans go awry when an employer falls on hard times, relocates your job, or offers bum benefits. Or the setback might be a government policy or regulation, or even a change in the tax code.

Whether the threat to your wealth comes in the form of a person, entity, policy, employer, or your own human nature, your best defense is vigilance. Watch where you're going. Be ready to use the brake as well as the throttle. If you stay alert to any trouble in your path, you are far more likely to move full speed ahead to financial independence.

CHAPTER 14

THE BIGGEST THREAT OF ALL

We humans can be our own worst enemies when it comes to financial planning. Emotions get in the way of rational decision making. Our own limiting beliefs and perceptions hold us back, often because we don't recognize them.

T ed and Janet loved their new house. They had done well in their careers and had saved and invested responsibly. This was their gift to themselves for retirement: a $1.5 million lakeside estate. The purchase was quite a stretch, even for their relatively healthy portfolio, but it represented their dream. They had waited for the day when they could have a beautiful house and the freedom to travel.

As any homeowner knows, repairs and improvements can soon add up to a major expense. And touring the world doesn't come cheap. Ted and Janet didn't hold back on either. They spent and spent, right up to when the housing market began to crash.

Surely this had to be a blip on the screen, they told themselves. No reason to panic. They reassured each other that their $1.5 million investment was bound to keep growing. Look at how lovingly they had cared for it!

Before long, though, Ted and Janet found themselves so over-extended, they were saying what they *really* had wanted all along was a smaller house that wouldn't tie them down. Maybe it was time to cash in their investment and use the equity for something more appropriate to their wanderlust lifestyle.

"Let's find out how much we could get for it," Janet suggested to her husband one day after they had been browsing through brochures for a Tahiti cruise. Off they went to a real estate agent, who combed through the comps, crunched the numbers, and recommended an asking price of $1.2 million, for starters. "We might still get a taker at that price, if we can get the place to appraise," she told them. They walked out. This wasn't happening.

So they waited until they could wait no more. No magic fix came along, and so Ted and Janet, finally, listed their dream house for sale. They had no rush of prospective buyers outbidding one another in their living room. Nobody plunked down $2 million in cash—nor a million. They ended up selling it for about $800,000.

"Well, I suppose it's better than nothing," Janet remarked as she and her husband signed the papers at the closing. Sure. But it was about half what they had paid. The house hadn't come close to the money-making investment they envisioned—quite the opposite. Much of their life savings had vanished.

Getting Out of Your Own Way

Countless homeowners became their own worst enemies during the housing crisis, which surfaced in 2007 and worsened in the ensuing recessionary years. They couldn't accept the failure of an "investment" so dear to their hearts and souls; but one can stay underwater only so long before drowning.

Homeowners have a way of letting their emotions get the better of them. They buy into the dream and tend to spend too much—and why not? Everyone says the house will grow in value. It might, but it very well might not. Saddled with a mortgage, they then face the onslaught of property taxes and insurance, lawn care and repairs, furniture and furnishings, upkeep and updates. The house can become more like a black hole than an investment. I have often heard a version of this: "We're going to spend $150,000 on renovations, and we'll get that money back!" No, you won't.

Making that decision based on unbridled emotion was Ted and Janet's first mistake. They had worked hard and felt entitled. Then, they imagined that a house was some sort of mint rather than a place to live. Even the spiraling housing market didn't dispel their deeply ingrained illusion, so they held on to the bitter end. That was their next mistake—letting their emotions blind them. They had poured so much money into the house they couldn't give up now, they told themselves. And when they finally did have to give up, they still wanted to look on the bright side. But there was no bright side.

Ted and Janet, in effect, could not get out of their own way. The biggest threat to their wealth was themselves. Their experience serves as a case study in the science of behavioral finance—namely, the principles of confirmation bias, anchoring, sunk costs, and selective memory that are among the human traits that can lead to poor money decisions. The field of behavioral finance is relatively new but has become widely recognized. It has been the specialty of two winners of the Nobel Prize for economics: Daniel Kahneman in 2002 and Richard Thaler in 2017.

In this chapter, we will examine several emotional obstacles to financial independence.

You may recognize some of the inner forces that have been driving your spending, saving, and investment decisions. Remember, knowledge is power. Through awareness, you can overcome the negative forces that don't serve you.

HARMFUL BEHAVIOR BIASES	
Market timing	Sunk cost
Overconfidence	Anchoring
Self-handicapping	Confirmation bias
Selective memory	Mental accounting
Loss aversion	Herding

MARKET TIMING

Investors often try to "time the market" by jumping in and out of it based on their desire for greater gains or their fear of greater losses. They get greedy when the market is advancing, and they panic when it is retreating.

Greed and fear, however, are primal emotions, and they get in the way of rational thinking. That's why so many investors buy high and sell low. They ignore the bargains and wait till the price has been marked up several times before buying. That's a good way to lose money. They wouldn't think of doing that in the supermarket, but it's how they invest in the stock market.

"I got out of the market in 2008 just before the crash," a visitor to my office declared. He smiled, proud of his prowess. To which I replied, "Great! When did you get back in?" He didn't. He avoided one of history's worst recessions, but he missed out on one of history's strongest recoveries. The point is this: not only do you have to get the exit right, you also have to get the entry right, and that can be next to impossible, even for the pros.

OVERCONFIDENCE

One investor reads a blog about an up-and-coming security and rushes to buy it, feeling in his bones that he is making the right move—a case of overconfidence. Another investor proudly declares that she goes strictly by the numbers. "I'm not emotional," she says. "I did a spreadsheet and all the analysis. This stock is a winner if I ever saw one!" But has she examined every single variable? Her sense of certainty seems unfounded. This, too, is a case of overconfidence.

A widely cited study found that 93 percent of drivers rated themselves as better than the median.[7] If most drivers think they are better than average, then half of them clearly are wrong. Likewise, a lot of people falsely believe they are above par in evaluating the market. Optimism is fine, but don't be naive. The market has a way of humbling those who think they can't go wrong.

Stock picking is a risky game. The experts get it wrong much of the time, and so will you unless you have a legitimate niche of expertise and insight that gives you a clear edge. If you can't make that claim, this isn't the game for you.

---

7   Ola Svenson, "Are We All Less Risky and More Skillful Than Our Fellow Drivers?," *Acta Psychologica* 47 (1981): 143–148.

SELF-HANDICAPPING

Self-handicapping is the flip side of overconfidence. It is the human tendency to concoct excuses for why things might not turn out well. Those who doubt their ability or don't want to put in the effort to succeed in an endeavor often will do and say things to protect their self-esteem in case they fail. A football quarterback, for example, complains before the big game that his elbow hurts, whether that's true or not. If he performs poorly, maybe it was because of that aching elbow. If he does great, it was despite that aching elbow.

Let's say an investor wants to buy a risky stock but doesn't check out the numbers. That's too much work. He knows, though, just what to say if the stock turns out to be a loser: "Well, I admit I didn't research that one as much as I usually do." In his mind, it's a good setup. He can still take credit if it works out, and if it doesn't, he can blame some circumstance that got in the way of his typical vigilance. It's far better to spend that time and energy doing things right in the first place.

SELECTIVE MEMORY

A well-known principle of psychology is cognitive dissonance or inconsistency in one's thoughts, beliefs, or attitudes. People feel compelled to correct that inconsistency by selectively remembering how an event of the past played out. Ted and Janet, for example, were remembering selectively as they tried to see the bright side in their house debacle.

Investors often try to put their poor choices in a positive light. If you think of yourself as wise at picking securities, how do you explain a blunder from long ago? Many people would rationalize it as not so bad after all. They tell themselves they sold before the worst happened, or they were just going by the best information anyone had at the time. Over the years, they increasingly distort the truth of what happened. But people are supposed to learn from mistakes, not transform them into victories.

LOSS AVERSION

Psychologists have long observed that people tend to feel the pain of a loss more strongly than the pleasure of a gain. *They hate to lose more than they love to win.* That principle of loss aversion often plays into investment decisions. As a stock sinks in value, investors often hang on tight for far too long. Averse to losing, they tell themselves it's still a winner but just going through a bad patch. That mind-set keeps them stuck in a rut when they should be moving on. Opportunities might beckon elsewhere, but they care more about trying to keep what they have.

SUNK COST

When you have been sinking a lot of money into something—your house, for example—it can be hard to stop that spending even when it feels more like bleeding. You can't get that money back, so you hope for the best despite your doubts. Homeowners often do that. Ted and Janet kept throwing good money after bad, even as the market was draining the value of their house.

Sometimes it's not a matter of money. People often keep plugging away at a losing endeavor or relationship; they have already put so much time and effort into it. That's a cost, too, and it can keep people from facing up to the tough decisions they need to make.

Sunk costs can motivate people to stick with a good decision as well. Let's say Jill has spent months saving for a vacation that her family has been joyfully anticipating. She puts down a large, nonrefundable deposit. Two weeks before the trip, her employer lays her off, and Jill needs to scramble to find a new job. If she had won that trip in a sweepstakes, she probably would have canceled it. But she chooses to go. Why? Because her money is on the line. For better or for worse, people think twice about sacrificing their own hard-earned dollars.

ANCHORING

Call it stubborn or call it determined, it is also quite human: once people make up their mind about what something should be worth, they often don't want to budge from it despite evidence to the contrary. Ted and Janet refused to accept that their house was worth anything less than the $1.5 million they paid for it. Their reaction demonstrates the psychological principle of anchoring. It is the tendency to hold fast to an initial piece of information and use it as a benchmark for making decisions.

Anchoring is common among investors. After a big loss, for example, an investor will try to get back to break even, even if it takes a decade to return to that high-water mark. Or an investor might jump to buy a stock that has suddenly fallen from a recent high, seeing the dip as a bargain. By anchoring on that former high, the investor cannot see that the dip is actually a symptom of a company in deep trouble.

Couples planning for retirement often anchor by telling themselves they need, say, a million dollars before they can take that big step. Thirty years later, that remains their goal, but now they will need twice that. To get the same buying power that $1 million would have given them in 1988, the couple would need $2.1 million in 2018.

CONFIRMATION BIAS

Confirmation bias is the tendency to look for information that supports what you already believe or have decided to do. You want to buy a house or change jobs, and so you look for the information and seek out the advice that confirms it's a good idea. That's part of the reason Ted and Janet spent too much on their dream house: You simply can't lose when it comes to real estate, right? Wrong, of course, but nobody told them that, or if anyone did, they weren't listening.

MENTAL ACCOUNTING

When people gamble, they are much more likely to take a greater risk with money they have won because they perceive it as house money. In their mental accounting, it is something extra they can afford to blow.

Similarly, people look at an income tax refund as found money. Instead of carefully budgeting it, they use it to buy themselves something special. It's not a gift. They're getting back their own money because they set too much aside, but they don't see it that way.

Mental accounting can be good or bad. Putting money into different "buckets," depending on how you intend to use it, can be wise. You certainly should keep your retirement money distinct from the money you are saving to buy a car, and you should be investing each of those accounts differently depending on whether the money is for a short-term or long-term goal. Too many buckets and too much complexity, though, can confuse matters. In finance, there is no such thing as house money. It's not extra. You earned it, and you should invest or save or spend it as wisely as any other dollar.

Ultimately, you want to put all your money to its best use. Does it make sense, for example, to stuff money into a piggy bank for a vacation fund when you are carrying a ton of credit card debt? If you are going to tally your money for different purposes, do so in a way that most efficiently moves you toward financial independence.

HERDING

First came the dot-com bubble that burst at the turn of the millennium. Then we saw the bubble in the housing market as investors fled from tech stocks to what they perceived to be a safer asset class. That one burst, too, inaugurating the Great Recession.

Those were recent events. History has seen a variety of such irrational asset surges as investors followed the madding crowd. In Holland, the tulip mania of 1636 saw prices soar twentyfold before utterly collapsing, all in the space of six months. In 1720, British investors rushed to buy shares in the South Sea Company, lured by the directors' tales of untold wealth. That bubble also burst within a year.[8]

It's an indisputable phenomenon of economic behavior: investors tend to run with the herd. They decide that the latest hot idea is better than a time-tested principle, and they fear being left behind as the crowd hustles past. Whether it's greed or an innate human desire to conform, it can add up to disastrous decision making.

---

8   Harvard Business School, "South Sea Bubble Short History," Baker Library, accessed February 4, 2019, https://www.library.hbs.edu/hc/ssb/history.html.

The Antidote to Emotions

If you are unaware of the role your emotions can play in your financial life, your biggest risk is *you*. You can get in your own way to the point at which you block your chances for financial independence and an enjoyable life.

The antidote to those emotions is the rational advice of an independent advisor who can shortstop the mistakes you risk making. All athletes need a coach to help bring out the best in them. Every sports team needs the same: someone with an independent point of view to develop strategies for success. And you need a coach, too, to help you with your financial plan for life.

> **If you are unaware of the role your emotions can play in your financial life, your biggest risk is *you*.**

Each of us has substantial potential within, but we can sabotage ourselves if we fail to curb the human tendencies and behaviors that can lead us down the wrong paths. Along the way are many pitfalls, and a good guide can help you step around them. Learn as much as you can, while you can, about investing for life. You are building a legacy, and it consists of more than money. You also will be passing to the next generations the knowledge you have gained on your journey—so learn those lessons well.

PART FIVE

. . .

CREATE A LEGACY YOU LOVE

As people get older, they ponder how much money they will leave to heirs and how much to charity. Estate planning and philanthropic planning offer solutions, combining the ethereal with the practical: Which causes are worthy, who gets what and how much, and how taxes factor in?

CHAPTER 15

DON'T LEAVE A MESS FOR YOUR HEIRS

Even if you do not consider yourself wealthy, you need an estate plan. Thoughtful preparation ensures that your money will pass smoothly to your heirs. Without a good plan, you could leave behind a lot of heartache.

'll call them the Smiths and the Joneses, common names to represent common scenarios that couples face when either the husband or the wife dies. Mr. and Mrs. Jones did nothing to streamline how they would leave their assets. Mr. and Mrs. Smith worked out the details well in advance. I wish I could say I have seen more of the latter among those who come to see me, but more often than not, the family is left with a financial nightmare.

Though I've changed the names, these two stories are essentially real, and all four of those people died within eighteen months of one another. In the Smith family, the children could feel a sense of peace, even in the depths of mourning, knowing that everything was in place for a smooth transition. In the Jones family, the children had to untangle a financial mess and spend hours getting matters settled. Their tears of grief were mixed with tears of frustration.

The bright side of this tale involves the Smiths, whose daughter and son-in-law had been my clients for years. Relatively early in their retirement, the couple came to see me, and with time still on our side, we set to work on a full range of planning, including their wills, trusts, and health care power of attorney. Eventually, the husband passed away before his wife, which often happens. The estate plan was designed to function well, no matter which spouse died first. When the time came, all the assets transferred smoothly to eighty-five-year-old Mrs. Smith, with minimal probate hassle and costs. It wasn't long before she passed, too, and the couple's two children inherited their money without an administrative mess or contention between them. We had orchestrated in advance how it all would play out, allowing for a variety of contingencies.

Not so for the Joneses. Their son came to my office to introduce himself and tell me his mother was on her deathbed and his father had done no estate planning. We immediately began getting documents in order, meeting with her in the hospital. However, she passed away quickly, before we could get anything in place. Her husband was not cooperating. An aging military veteran, he had run his family in an authoritarian manner. He didn't want any help, and he didn't want anyone knowing much about the couple's financial affairs—and that had included his wife. He figured she didn't need to know because he took care of her. She was not financially sophisticated, and she was fully dependent on him, never having had her own career. He relished that feeling of control over life and finances, and he hadn't shared any details with their children, either.

When his son came to see me, he didn't know where to start. His father had presumed he would die first, the son told me, but that was not how it was playing out. To complicate matters immensely, the father was showing signs of dementia, which would worsen in the months ahead as he struggled to go on alone. Even if he had been willing to relinquish control, he no longer was competent to deal with finances, or with much of anything else. Within a matter of months, he died, too, without any planning or estate documents in place.

As it turned out, the father had put $1 million in a joint brokerage account with one of the children, an unwise but common move among older people who presume that the kid will do the right thing. The kid, as joint owner, gets everything, but doing what's right is a matter of perspective. When there are simmering grievances in a family, which so often happens, the siblings sometimes get nothing. In this case, they divvied up the money fairly, as their dad had intended, although the money now had to be gifted to the other siblings. Fortunately, it was possible to accomplish that gifting without exceeding the lifetime exemption on estate tax. As a result, the brothers and sisters got their portions free of taxes, but it required a much greater expenditure of time, effort, and lawyer fees than necessary.

It worked out, not ideally but satisfactorily, and with a great deal of anxiety. In many families, a feud would have ensued. Lingering resentments over estate matters can divide parent and child and brother and sister till the end of their days. That's what is at risk when families procrastinate on estate planning.

Neither of those families had an estate plan when I met them, but one was able to get a plan in place while the other waited too long to do anything effective. Taking care of just the basics can make a dramatic difference.

Everyone Needs a Plan

For many people, the concept of estate planning conjures images of lawyers combing through complex documents for wealthy clients and charging a hefty fee. In reality, estate planning can benefit virtually anyone, and my years of experience have shown me that the legal aspects, though important, are only a small part of it.

The bulk of estate planning is not legal in nature, and it should be accomplished before a lawyer gets involved. Some fundamental questions need to be answered first. In essence: What do you want to happen if something should happen to you? What are your goals?

Once you have set the direction and destination for the estate planning, then you can bring in the legal experts to make sure the documentation is in place to get you where you want to go.

The purpose of an estate plan is to determine what will become of the resources that you have put together during your lifetime, from the big picture down to who gets Mom's wedding ring. I have witnessed many family fights over rings and furniture and plates. The passing of a parent is a time of stress and grief, when family members are not necessarily at their best and raw emotions surface.

> **The purpose of an estate plan is to determine what will become of the resources that you have put together during your lifetime, from the big picture down to who gets Mom's wedding ring.**

If you develop a good estate plan, you can settle matters in advance and minimize conflict. You can also arrange to carry forward, after you are gone, the causes you have embraced and the goals you have set. If you should pass before your children go to college, for example, a well-crafted estate plan will keep that goal in place.

Virtually everyone has an estate, whether wealthy or not, and therefore everyone needs a plan for it. If you are taking the time to read this book, you likely have assets and interests that you will be passing on. If you have a home or personal property, investments, bank accounts, or business ownership, you have an estate, and therefore you need a plan.

The Three Components of an Estate Plan

Estate planning entails these three primary aims.

1. It should arrange to take care of you while you are living. If you become incapacitated, either mentally or physically, a good estate plan will arrange for your care and safeguard your interests when you cannot personally take care of yourself or your affairs.

2. Your estate plan arranges for the smooth transition of your possessions and assets after you die.

3. An estate plan addresses how you can take care of your kids, even when you can no longer be with them.

I once was asked for my advice in the case of an eighteen-year-old, Joey, whose parents had long since divorced and whose father, with whom he was living, had just passed away. Mom had her own struggles and couldn't help. Dad had done no estate planning and left major debts, so upon his death, all his possessions and bank accounts, including their house, went to satisfy those debts.

Joey, who had started at community college, was basically left homeless. In the eyes of the law, he was an adult who was responsible for finding his own way, though he was far from ready. Neither parent had been able to provide for his future. Fortunately, a relative took him in for a while. There wasn't much I could do. The estate planning should have commenced years earlier.

The point is this: families and friends and caring neighbors need to make arrangements. Who would have been Joey's guardian if his father had died a few years earlier? An estate plan can designate a guardian for juveniles, but Joey, though technically an adult, still needed guidance and nurturing. In such cases, families should anticipate well in advance how they will deal with such situations, and then formalize those decisions in writing.

Taking care of tomorrow is what estate planning aims to do for you and for your loved ones. Let's look closely at those three components of estate planning.

Taking Care of You and Your Assets

The basic estate-planning documents deal with carrying out your wishes for the distribution of your assets and designating someone to make decisions on your behalf, both financial and medical, if you cannot do so yourself. The rules can vary significantly from state to state, so what follows is a general overview. Some aspects of estate planning are federal, but others are specific to the states and even counties. Therefore, consult with an attorney licensed in your jurisdiction.

LAST WILL AND TESTAMENT

Your will is the essential document for designating how and to whom you wish to leave your assets, whether to heirs or to charity. You name an executor (or executrix or administrator) who files your will in probate court upon your death and then works with the court to distribute your assets as you have decreed, ensuring that all debts, expenses, and taxes get paid. Your will also names a guardian for juvenile children. Probate court records are public, and each state has its own procedures. Some still have inheritance taxes.

REVOCABLE LIVING TRUST

Unlike a will, which takes effect upon your passing, a revocable living trust can manage your affairs while you are alive if you can no longer do so. You can change its provisions at any time, so as long as you are capable, you can be your own trustee and keep managing your investments and financial affairs. If you become incapacitated, your designee becomes the trustee. After your death, the terms of the trust remain in force. You can stipulate exactly how to distribute your assets with provisions that can extend your influence for generations. Because you shifted your assets into a trust, they will not be subject to the lengthy, costly procedures of probate court, open to public perusal.

In short, having a revocable trust eases the management of your affairs. If you have property in several states, for example, your executor won't have to travel far and wide to probate your will in several courts. For anyone with substantial assets, a revocable living trust can go far toward ensuring that loved ones don't inherit a mess.

POWER OF ATTORNEY

This document gives a person of your choosing the authority to take care of your financial affairs, such as managing your investments and paying your bills. A "springing" power takes effect only when you become incapacitated; a "durable" power takes effect upon signing. Either way, you are granting a trustworthy individual the discretion to take care of your assets to the extent that you decide is appropriate. This power does not extend beyond your death.

HEALTH-CARE POWER OF ATTORNEY

If you become unable to make your own medical decisions, this specific durable power specifies someone who will have the authority to do so on your behalf. This document can spare families untold grief. Relatives often disagree on the best course of medical care, sometimes battling it out in court. You can settle the matter by choosing who decides.

ADVANCE MEDICAL DIRECTIVE

If you hate the thought of lingering unconscious on life support, be clear about your preferences for end-of-life care. In an advance medical directive, or "living will," you can state your desire not to be kept alive against your wishes. You file the document with your health care providers, who can abide by your wishes with less concern that they will be held liable. Unlike a health care power of attorney, however, this directive grants nobody the right to make decisions on your behalf.

HIPAA AUTHORIZATION

This document has become highly important in recent years under the privacy mandate of the Health Insurance Portability and Accountability Act (HIPAA) of 1996. Fearing fines and lawsuits, health care providers have clamped down on who can see medical records or discuss your condition with your medical providers. You need to designate which people will be allowed to receive your health care information if you become incapacitated and unable to speak for yourself. The person who has your health care power of attorney will have HIPAA authorization as well.

Deciding Who Will Get What

There is no standard way of distributing your property. However, if you die without a will, which is "intestate," or without a trust, the state will decide where your property goes and who gets what. The rules vary by state, but if you are married, your spouse usually will get some of the assets. If you have children, they will probably be entitled to a portion. If you have minor children, the state will decide who will take care of them. The court makes the decisions and issues orders that must be followed. That's why you should clearly outline your wishes in advance.

In drafting a will or the provisions of a trust, people often fear they would be showing favoritism if they left unequal portions of the estate to their beneficiaries. More important than being equal is being fair and considering the varying needs of the beneficiaries. Let's say you have a multibillionaire daughter who made a fortune in a tech startup, and you have a son who has a disability and will need care for life. Will you still leave your assets equally to each of those children? Some parents take the balanced approach, thinking they will prevent conflict. However, an unequal distribution could make sense for many good reasons. If you worry about a misunderstanding, explain your rationale in a letter left with your attorney or executor.

> **In drafting a will or the provisions of a trust, people often fear they would be showing favoritism if they left unequal portions of the estate to their beneficiaries. More important than being equal is being fair.**

Give some thought to whether you will be leaving money outright to your family and heirs or placing it in a trust for them. If you are in a second marriage, for example, property decisions become complicated, which can call for the provisions of a trust. The right kind of trust, if properly drafted, also can protect money from litigation and creditors.

The world has become overly litigious. If you leave all your money outright to your spouse, consider what could happen if someone were to sue over an auto accident. Your spouse could lose it all. In a properly drafted trust, the money would be out of bounds for a settlement.

A trust is also a wise choice if you believe an heir needs to mature before receiving an inheritance. You can draft provisions in a trust that control how and when anyone gets assets—upon reaching a certain age, for example, or enrolling in college, when buying a first house, or starting a business.

Taking Care of Your Children

Naming a guardian for your children in your will is a big decision. If something happens to you, that person will be responsible for feeding, clothing, housing, and educating them. That person will serve as a substitute parent, so be cautious in your choice. But do choose someone. I know people who frequently travel overseas on business, leaving their children with a caretaker until they return. You can imagine the complications if something were to happen to the parents and the children had no official guardian.

Young people often name their parents as guardians of their kids—but consider whether leaving a five-year-old child with your seventy-year-old parents is wise. Grown siblings are a natural choice, as well as close friends.

The guardian does not have to be the person who controls the money. You could name one person to be guardian and someone else to be the trustee of the children's trust, as sort of a check and balance. Just be sure not to create a financial hardship for the guardian—and if you have several children, that is a particularly big concern. Your trust provisions can spell out how money can be released in various situations. You are putting your money and the welfare of your children into the hands of your trustee and guardian, so choose wisely.

Other Considerations

Certain assets do not go through probate because the ownership has already been established. That is the case, for example, when an account is held jointly, or when a beneficiary has been listed to receive the money in a retirement account or the payout from an insurance policy. Most beneficiaries are spouses or family members, but you can name your trust or your estate as the beneficiary if you wish. However, don't do that without professional guidance, preferably from an experienced tax attorney. You could face consequences you did not anticipate.

Your estate planning should include a careful review of those beneficiaries and joint account holders. They are the people who will get those assets, no matter what you have declared in your will or trust provisions. A woman once came to see me after her husband died, saying she needed access to his IRA. I couldn't help her. She was not the beneficiary; he had not updated the listing, and his ex-wife was more than happy to stake her legal claim.

> **Your estate planning should include a careful review of those beneficiaries and joint account holders. They are the people who will get those assets, no matter what you have declared in your will or trust provisions.**

That has not been the only case where people have come to us seeking help. I have seen insurance policies paid to ex-wives as well. I saw an IRA go to a child that the parents had intended to disinherit. *People forget to change their beneficiaries.*

For all new clients, we conduct a careful review that prevents such a nightmare, but once the policyholder or account holder has died, there's no recourse.

Estate Taxes

While some states still impose estate taxes or inheritance taxes at lower levels of net worth, for most people the specter of estate taxes has vanished. A married couple would have to have over $22 million in assets before their estate would be subject to federal estate tax if they died in 2018. This high value doesn't eliminate the need for tax planning, but for many it has become much simpler.

The chart on the next page outlines key data points regarding the federal estate tax system going back to 2010.

YEAR	2010	2011	2012	2013	2014	2015	2016	2017	2018
ESTATE/ GIFT TAX EXEMPTION	$5 million	$5 million	$5.12 million	$5.2 million	$5.34 million	$5.43 million	$5.45 million	$5.49 million	$11.2 million
TAX RATE	35%	35%	35%	40%	40%	40%	40%	40%	40%
GST TAX EXEMPTION	$5 million	$5 million	$5.12 million	$5.2 million	$5.34 million	$5.43 million	$5.45 million	$5.49 million	$11.2 million
TAX RATE	0%	35%	35%	40%	40%	40%	40%	40%	40%
GIFT TAX ANNUAL EXCLUSION	$13,000	$13,000	$13,000	$14,000	$14,000	$14,000	$14,000	$14,000	$15,000

All figures are current as of 2018

A True Legacy

As you can see, estate planning involves a lot more than tax management. Many people cross estate planning off their to-do list because they figure it's something for the ultra-wealthy and so they don't need to worry about it. True, they might be exempt from the estate tax, but they are not exempt from leaving a mess in the variety of ways examined in this chapter.

Estate planning should not be a do-it-yourself undertaking. As your life circumstances change, seek professional guidance to help with the regular reviews and updates that are essential to protecting the interests of you and your family. Thoughtful and thorough preparation will yield an array of long-term benefits.

You can make a difference in your family for generations, and your charitable endeavors can extend your influence to bettering the world. That way, you *can leave a true legacy.*

CHAPTER 16

YOUR PHILANTHROPIC HEART

The desire to leave a legacy has led many people to philanthropic planning. It's a lot more than a way to reduce taxes, although it does that quite effectively. Your choice of charities reflects your values and your purpose in life.

T he two couples had enjoyed stellar careers and wanted to give back to their alma maters, but Brian and Rachel wanted to offer help in the here and now, while Jeff and Carol preferred to arrange an endowment for after they passed away.

As I was helping Brian and Rachel sell their private medical practice, they reminisced about their days in college, living on ramen noodles while pursuing their degrees. "We think of those as good times," Brian said, "but, man, it was a struggle. There were days when we were looking for spare change under the couch cushions, and it took years to pay off those loans."

Rachel nodded, and added, "We're doing well, but those days were tough going, and it's gotten worse for kids trying to make it now. We want to do something." They had been talking about sharing a portion of their good fortune with the university they had attended.

"It sounds as if you'd like to fund a scholarship," I said, "and maybe even tag it for a student in your field." They brightened at the idea. We set up an endowment in which they donated enough principal to generate sufficient interest every year to pay for the annual tuition of a medical student of the university's choosing. For their generosity, they got a big tax deduction. Each year, they felt the satisfaction of a young person's gratitude. They saw their philanthropy in action.

Jeff and Carol likewise wanted to give back, and they had saved responsibly. However, they now needed to invest all that money to produce an adequate retirement income for the rest of their lives. And what then? They had no children, so they had been wondering who would inherit their money. The couple had a heart for animals, regularly taking in strays from rescue centers. They had a heart for helping people, too, and so, as Brian and Rachel had done, they decided to fund a scholarship.

This endowment, though, would not be immediate, since Jeff and Carol needed the money while they were alive. Their legacy would come afterward, when, each year, a veterinary student would be able to go to classes, thanks to their endowment. As part of their charitable planning, I helped them work out the most efficient way to leave their money so it could continue to help others for many years.

A Celebration of Life

Why am I here? Why do I walk the earth? Such questions often arise as people get older and can slow down long enough to contemplate the meaning of life. They often want to leave a legacy of some sort. A common perception is that philanthropic planning is mostly about tax strategies, and it is true that the savings can be significant. But it is, foremost, an act of benevolence. The tax benefits exist to encourage and reward charitable donations.

Philanthropic planning isn't a prelude to dying. It's for the here and now. It should be pursued in the spirit of celebrating life, not anticipating death. If you have been blessed with all you need and more, you can become a blessing to others today. But whether you give now or upon your passing, think of it as the fulfillment of a goal. If leaving a meaningful legacy matters to you, then you will want to support the causes or institutions you cherish.

> **A common perception is that philanthropic planning is mostly about tax strategies, and it is true that the savings can be significant. But it is, foremost, an act of benevolence.**

Otherwise, Uncle Sam will be happy to partake of more of your money, spending it as he wishes, and you will become a philanthropist nonetheless—an involuntary one. Most people would rather have more control than that, so they engage in both short- and long-term strategies that preserve their ability to say who gets what.

To talk about philanthropy in terms of tax strategies is not cynical; it's simply sensible. We give our tithes and other regular donations because it is the right thing to do. We're not necessarily motivated by the tax savings. Nonetheless, we do get the deductions each year as a short-term benefit. When we decide to give on a larger scale, we can get a longer-term benefit, but we still are choosing charities that reflect our values.

Giving Now or Giving Later

Once you have decided to donate, select a method that is appropriate for your situation. The fundamental question is whether you are able to give while you are alive or need to keep that money for now and donate it upon your passing. Either way requires thoughtful planning. Several vehicles are available to help you meet your goals for short-term or long-term giving. Choose the ones that will serve your purpose most efficiently, saving you the most so you can give more.

As shown in Chapter 15, starting in 2018, families are getting twice the exemption from the federal estate tax than they had previously received. Through at least 2025, they will pay a tax only on the value of an estate that exceeds $11.18 million for an individual or $22.36 million for a married couple. In addition, the annual gift tax exemption was raised by $1,000. Thus, an individual taxpayer is excused from filing a gift tax return on amounts up to $15,000 per recipient each year; for couples, it's $30,000 per recipient, free of tax, and free of paperwork. If you give somebody more than that, the excess amount isn't immediately taxable; it's simply deducted from your available lifetime estate-tax exemption. With the doubling of that exemption, far fewer taxpayers need worry about depleting their exemption.

Nonetheless, be aware. Some states maintain their own exemption levels. Always know the tax regulations that affect you at all levels of government and understand that you could face tax consequences when you give money away.

Since early in my financial career, I have been involved in a program run by the US Department of Veterans Affairs. This program gives free financial counseling to the beneficiaries, mostly widows, of soldiers who die with an active serviceman's group life insurance policy in place.

Around the turn of the millennium, I met a widow whose husband was killed in Iraq. She was in the military, too, in Afghanistan. They had been married only a year and never truly had the opportunity to start a life together. She got life insurance payouts on both a military and a commercial policy. Feeling guilty about getting all that money, she gave a portion of the money to her deceased husband's parents.

"It's like giving to charity, right?" said the young widow as I reviewed her situation. "They needed that money more than I did! Don't I get to write that off my taxes or something?" I told her the sad reality. It was a generous gift, and I understood her largesse and compassion, but she had created a tax issue for herself. The federal lifetime exemption back then was only about $650,000, and at the time, North Carolina had its own tax (which it has since repealed) on gifts exceeding about $100,000. She hadn't realized the consequences of her "charity," and it was too late to restructure it.

The lessons are clear: *when you are giving money away, understand the implications at all levels of government.* If you are giving money to family members, understand that those gifts will not be treated as charitable contributions and you will get no tax deductions. Under some circumstances, as we have seen, you could even owe tax.

Simple Strategies

Donating to a charity can be as simple as writing a check, but you can make an outright gift in more tax-efficient ways.

A simple strategy is to donate stock that has significantly appreciated in value. One approach would be to sell that stock, pay the capital gains tax on the appreciation, and write a check to the charity for whatever amount remains. Many people do it that way, but a much better approach would be to donate the stock directly. The charity, as a tax-exempt entity, could then sell the stock itself without incurring any taxes. It would keep the entire value. Meanwhile, you get a tax deduction for your contribution.

That simple principle also applies when donating real estate. If you sell the property yourself, you will be taxed on its gain in value. If you donate it directly, you can deduct the value of your gift, and the charity can sell the property free of taxes. While the IRS limits how much can be deducted for different types of gifts in any one year, excess contributions can generally be carried forward and used in subsequent years.

You also can give to charity via your will or revocable trust. You can either specify a dollar amount or set the donation as a percentage of the estate's value. Some people designate a percentage of the residuals. For example, the deceased spouse's will designates that the surviving spouse gets the first $5 million, and of the remainder, 10 percent goes to charity.

You could structure such provisions in a wide variety of ways such as setting up contingencies. For example, you designate that upon your death, all your money goes to your spouse and children, but if none of them is alive at that point, it all goes to charity. That sort of provision is typical among younger people, who tend to put family first. Older people whose children have grown are more likely to give priority to charities, particularly after a spouse has died.

Life insurance is a simple tool for giving money. Consider these two strategies:

1. Make an irrevocable gift of the policy to a charity. If complete ownership is transferred to the nonprofit and the

charity is named as the beneficiary, the gift will generate a charitable income tax deduction, but how much is somewhat complicated.

2.   Name the charity as the primary or contingent beneficiary of the policy. This will not produce an income tax charitable deduction for the payment of future premiums on the policy, but it does afford the donor a full estate-tax charitable deduction when the donor dies.

Another simple tool is a "pay on death" or "transfer on death" account. To set it up, put on record with your bank or broker that the money in an account is to go to a specific charity at the time of your death. You can specify a charitable bequest for the assets in your 401(k) as well, although spousal consent is necessary. It also may be necessary for IRA assets, depending on state and community property laws.

Sophisticated Strategies

You may find that family members don't share your enthusiasm for leaving a lot of money to charity. To ease their minds, consider a trust. Charitable trusts fall into two main categories, depending on whether the charity gets its benefit now or later. They will either

1.   pay income to the charity for a set period, with the principal then reverting to the beneficiaries, called a charitable lead trust (CLT) or

2.   pay income to the beneficiaries for a set period, with the remainder then going to the charity, typically either a charitable remainder annuity trust (CRAT) or a charitable remainder unitrust (CRUT).

In the CRAT or CRUT arrangements, you can donate the assets to the trust for an immediate tax deduction but continue to manage those assets and receive an income from them for a specified period. You could use that income to help fund your retirement, or—so those family members don't feel disinherited—arrange for them to get the income for a set number of years. Afterward, the charity gets the remainder of the money.

You choose a time frame and structure that works best for your family while weighing the tax ramifications. Most large charities have attorneys or experts on staff to help design a strategy, and they often will pay the legal fees to draft the documents. A qualified advisor can fill you in on the details.

Another useful tool is a qualified charitable distribution (QCD). If you have an IRA, you must begin withdrawing money each year starting at age seventy and a half—whether you need the money or not. The government won't wait any longer to start collecting those long-deferred income taxes. However, the IRS now allows you to satisfy that annual requirement by transferring IRA assets directly to charities, which receive them free of tax. That's a smart way to give if you are so inclined and able to do so.

If you want to support multiple charities, you can do it efficiently through a single account known as a donor advised fund (DAF). You can fund the account now but hold off on distributions until later, managing it so you get your tax deductions during your high-income years when you need them most. A DAF is like having your own family foundation on a small scale, and it simplifies your giving. You and your family can meet each year to decide which charities you want to support, if any. Although the money must all go to charity eventually, you continue to control how it is invested. Your record keeping is all in one place, easily tracked. And you no longer have to fill out multiple forms for each small donation.

The charts on the following pages offer several options to consider in your charitable planning, depending on your goals.

The Simple Truth

Philanthropic planning need not become overly complex and involve a lot of attorney and accounting fees. When drafting complex trusts and other instruments, you must consult with a lawyer, of course, but know that a lot of low-cost solutions are available for tax-efficient giving.

An experienced advisor can help you decide on appropriate amounts to leave to your children and to charity—and when. The advisor will explain the various tools that would best serve your purposes.

The big step is getting started. Many people do not know whether philanthropy is possible for them. That often is because they are unclear about their own needs, and when in doubt, they understandably feel less generous. They hesitate to attend to the needs of others for fear of cutting themselves short. In their view, wealth is like a pie. A bigger slice for the charity means a smaller slice for them. But why not bake a bigger pie so that all

Remember the simple truth of why you are giving. Having succeeded, you want to help others succeed. Having been blessed yourself, you wish to bless others.

involved get more than their fill? Philanthropic planning aims to bake that bigger pie.

Remember the simple truth of why you are giving. Having succeeded, you want to help others succeed. Having been blessed yourself, you wish to bless others. Through philanthropy, you can make your mark on the world. It's why you walk the earth.

GIFT PLANNING POSSIBILITIES

	OPTION ONE	OPTION TWO	OPTION THREE	OPTION FOUR
IF YOU WOULD LIKE TO...	Make a significant future gift without affecting your current lifestyle	Make a significant gift to a charity with little or no cost to you or your family.	Find a tax-advantaged way to leave your assets to a charity and to your heirs upon your death.	Support a charity without depleting your cash reserves and avoid capital gains tax.
THEN CONSIDER...	A charitable bequest.	A life-insurance policy.	Naming a charity as a beneficiary of your retirement plan.	A gift of appreciated stock.
HOW YOU MAY BENEFIT...	Reduce estate and death taxes, and retain control over your assets during your lifetime.	Receive an immediate income tax deduction and possible future tax deductions through gifts made to pay policy premiums.	Avoid income tax on retirement plan assets, while making other property available to pass to your heirs.	Provide support to a charity while decreasing the out-of-pocket cost to you by avoiding capital gain tax.

GIFT PLANNING POSSIBILITIES

	OPTION FIVE	OPTION SIX	OPTION SEVEN	OPTION EIGHT
IF YOU WOULD LIKE TO...	Make a significant future gift to a charity and retain a fixed stream of income.	Make a significant gift to a charity and retain a variable stream of income.	Make a significant ongoing gift to a charity now and provide for your heirs later.	Make a significant gift to a charity without depleting your cash reserves and avoid capital gains tax.
THEN CONSIDER...	A charitable gift annuity.	A charitable trust.	A charitable lead trust.	A gift of real estate.
HOW YOU MAY BENEFIT...	Receive a current income stream and an immediate income tax deduction.	Receive a variable income stream and an immediate income tax deduction and avoid capital gains tax.	Reduce gift and estate taxes and dictate the timely passage of the gift to your heirs.	Deduct the fair-market value of the real estate for federal income-tax purposes and avoid capital gains tax.

CONCLUSION

THROUGH THE SEASONS

A frustrating aspect of my rewarding career has been trying to communicate clearly and succinctly what I do for a living. *What is a financial planner?*

Many people presume I'm a stockbroker or some sort of investment guru. But I'm not out to sell anything. I don't pick and trade individual stocks. I don't have an opinion on what the market did today or will do tomorrow, and I don't prognosticate on what's coming up in the economy. Rather, my overarching purpose is to help people manage their lives—to assist them in converting their human capital into passive income in an efficient, tax-advantaged, purposeful way.

To do that, I must get to know them. Much depends on developing relationships that can endure for years because they're built on trust. In my two decades of helping people with their financial plans, I have seen them advance through the seasons of life. I have seen their children grow into adults with their own families. I have seen new retirees venture out to see the world, not slowing down even in their eighties. And I have seen all the stages in between.

I have found great satisfaction in helping men and women build fulfilling lives based on the principles I have shared in these chapters. I have watched them invest their time, talents, and treasures into the pursuits that matter most to them. I have helped them make the right turns on their journey to financial independence.

Financial planning is indeed a journey, not an event. Even in the time I have been writing this book, laws, and therefore strategies, have been changing.

Opportunities and challenges come to each of us. How we deal with them is the measure of us. We do our best to get things right and set things right, but, at times, we fall short. What matters is how well we learn from our experiences and build for our betterment. That means we must set clear goals and devote ourselves to reaching them. As we mature, we recognize we don't need more stuff; we need more substance. And in our gratitude to a good life, we reach out to help others.

> Financial planning is indeed a journey, not an event. Even in the time I have been writing this book, laws, and therefore strategies, have been changing.

As for me, I am grateful for my parents and siblings whose love nurtured me, for the West Point staff and faculty who fostered my leadership skills, for my US Army Ranger and Special Operations comrades who molded me into a man, and for the many clients I have been honored to serve. I am grateful for the wonderful and selfless woman who agreed to share my life, and for the children we have ushered into the world.

And, yes, I am even grateful for that errant elk on Mount Rainier that crossed my path and repurposed my career. My soldier days had to end, but those enduring values of vigilance, preparation, loyalty, and patient endurance have stayed with me in my financial planning profession. In that way, I will be a soldier till my dying day.

It's time to invest in life, friends. That is the task before us. The portfolios do matter, the money matters, and all those strategies we have defined and redefined in these pages are important pieces to the puzzle.

But your puzzle needs to be assembled and solved. You must put together the life you desire, the one that will be meaningful to you and that will make a difference to your family, your community, and your world. Let's do it right.

WHAT YOU SHOULD DO TODAY

Here are eight steps you can take today as you invest in your life and build toward financial independence. If you commit to them, you will be off to a great start.

1. Change your mind-set from *building a portfolio* to *building a life.*

2. Set goals for where you want to go in life.

3. Invest in yourself. Design a plan to maximize your human capital.

4. Develop an investment strategy; don't just collect assets.

5. Identify threats to your wealth and actively work to mitigate them.

6. Make a plan to leave a meaningful legacy.

7. Hire a fee-only advisor to guide you in creating the life you envision.

8. Enjoy the journey and proceed with gratitude.

APPENDIX

MAJOR CHANGES OF THE TAX CUT AND JOBS ACT (TCJA) OF 2017 AFFECTING INDIVIDUALS

TAX RATES AND BRACKETS

Under the TCJA there will be seven tax brackets: 10, 12, 22, 24, 32, 35, and 37 percent. The top bracket starts at $600,000 of taxable income for married filing jointly, $300,000 for married filing separately, and $400,000 for single filers.

CAPITAL GAINS RATES AND NET INVESTMENT INCOME TAX

Tax rates on qualified dividend income, capital gains, and the 3.8 percent net investment income tax remain the same. However, the breakpoints between the 0, 15, and 20 percent rate no longer follow the tax brackets for regular income tax purposes.

PERSONAL EXEMPTIONS AND STANDARD DEDUCTION

The personal exemption deduction is repealed for all taxpayers and dependents under TCJA, but the standard deduction nearly doubles to $24,000 for married filing jointly taxpayers and $12,000 for single and married filing separately taxpayers.

CHILD TAX CREDIT

The TCJA increases the child tax credit to $2,000—$1,400 of which is refundable. The modified adjusted gross income threshold where the credit phases out is $400,000 for joint filers and $200,000 for all others. A new, nonrefundable tax credit of $500 was instituted for dependent children over the age of sixteen and all other dependents.

PASS-THROUGH TAX BREAK

Qualified business income from sole proprietorships, S corporations, partnerships, and LLCs taxed as partnerships are afforded a new 20 percent deduction under Section 199A. The deduction is claimed by individuals on their personal tax returns as a reduction to taxable income. This deduction is subject to a number of complicated restrictions and limitations above certain income amounts and for specific business types.

DEDUCTION FOR STATE AND LOCAL TAXES

There is now a $10,000 limit on the deduction for state and local taxes, including property, income, or sales taxes in lieu of income taxes.

MORTGAGE INTEREST DEDUCTION

Under TJCA, the limit on the loan amount for which a mortgage interest deduction can be claimed is reduced to $750,000, although existing loans are grandfathered. TCJA also repeals the deduction for interest on home equity loans unless used to buy, build, or substantially improve one's main residence.

DEDUCTION FOR MEDICAL EXPENSES

TCJA retains the deduction for unreimbursed medical expenses and, for 2017 and 2018, lowers the adjusted gross income (AGI) floor for claiming the deduction from 10 percent to 7.5 percent.

DEDUCTION FOR CASUALTY AND THEFT LOSSES

Except for losses incurred in presidentially declared disaster areas, TCJA repeals the deduction for casualty and theft losses.

DEDUCTION FOR CHARITABLE CONTRIBUTIONS

TCJA increases the maximum contribution percentage limit from 50 percent of a taxpayer's contribution base to 60 percent for cash contributions to public charities.

DEDUCTION FOR CERTAIN MISCELLANEOUS EXPENSES

TCJA repeals the deduction for any miscellaneous itemized deductions subject to 2 percent of the AGI floor.

REPEAL OF ALIMONY DEDUCTION

Effective for tax years beginning in 2019, the deduction for alimony paid and the corresponding inclusion in income by the recipient are repealed. Taxpayers who entered into agreements prior to 2019 will generally be grandfathered under the old rules.

ALTERNATIVE MINIMUM TAX (AMT)

The AMT exemption amounts are increased significantly to $70,300 for single taxpayers, $109,400 for married taxpayers, and $54,700 for married filing separately taxpayers. The phased-out limits are also raised. They start at $1,000,000 for married filing jointly and $500,000 for all others. These amounts are indexed each year for inflation after 2018.

PLAN DISTRIBUTIONS

Under TCJA, taxpayers may now use up to $10,000 in aggregate 529 distributions per year for elementary and secondary school tuition.
Repeal of Individual Healthcare Mandate
TCJA repeals the tax penalty on individuals under the Affordable Care Act (ACA) effective January 1 of 2019.

ESTATE AND GIFT TAX EXCLUSION

While the TCJA did not repeal the estate and gift tax, it permanently doubled the exclusion amount to $11.2 million and will still be indexed for inflation.

BLUESKY WEALTH
ADVISORS SERVICES

Dear Reader,

Congratulations you've made it through the entire book. Or maybe you skipped to the end to see how it turns out. Whichever path you took to get here, I'm glad you did. My purpose in authoring this book was purely to educate and train people how to become financially independent. For many of you with the time and inclination, you can take the knowledge presented here, combine it with hard work and the passage of time, and you can succeed financially.

I realize, though, that for some of you, your situation may be too complex, or you don't have the time required to plan and monitor all areas of your financial life adequately. I designed my firm, BlueSky Wealth Advisors, with you in mind.

We've put together a fantastic team of advisors and paired it with my twenty-plus years of understanding to create a client experience and menu of services that takes the heavy lifting off your plate and allows you to enjoy the fruits of building and maintaining wealth.

When you put this book down, don't fall back into the trap of busyness and procrastination. Take action today to improve your financial well-being! As you probably figured out from the book, I look at the world through a little bit different lens than most people. Part of my philosophy is this: **if you want to end up with above average finances, you have to do something different than the average person.** Just taking the first step to finding a fee-only fiduciary advisor to help guide you along the path to financial independence will set you apart from the crowd. As General George S. Patton said, "A good plan violently executed now is better than a perfect plan executed next week." Don't wait for the perfect time to get moving.

As a reader of my book, I'd like to extend a personal invitation to visit my company's website, www.blueskywa.com. There you will find a wealth of information on the services and philosophy of BlueSky as well as updated articles and guidance on our blog. While on the site be sure to visit the "Contact Us" page. If you let us know you are a reader of *Invest in Your Life, Not Just Your Portfolio*, we'll be happy to send you our newsletter, special client articles, and other exclusive content. You can also schedule a complimentary "Get Acquainted" session to find out more about BlueSky and see if we are a good match to be your trusted advisor.

Thanks again for reading and start today investing in your life.

Sincerely,

David L. Blain, CFA

avid L. Blain, CFA is the chief executive officer and senior wealth advisor at BlueSky Wealth Advisors, a fee-only, independent registered investment advisor (RIA) he founded in 1999. He is responsible for defining the overall firm policies, strategy, and goals. He also formulates advanced financial planning, sophisticated tax and estate strategies for clients, and is responsible for setting the firm-wide investment strategy.

David received a bachelor of science degree in 1989 from The United States Military Academy at West Point, where he was a Distinguished Honor Graduate and member of the Phi Kappa Phi Honor Society. Before his career in finance, he served with distinction for ten years in US Army Airborne, Ranger, and Special Operations units.

He is a member of the CFA Institute, the National Association of Personal Financial Advisors (NAPFA), and the Financial Planning Association (FPA). He currently serves on the Board of Directors of CarolinaEast Health System in New Bern, where he chairs the Investment Committee. Previously, David was on the Board of Advisors and Finance Committee of the West Point Association of Graduates. He was also treasurer of Big Brothers Big Sisters of Southeastern North Carolina, president of the Cumberland Interfaith Hospitality Network, and treasurer of the board for Catholic Charities of the Diocese of Raleigh. He served as the chairman of the New Bern Heart Ball and has provided countless hours of volunteer service to numerous other charitable organizations. In addition to his many board duties, he has coached youth and teen baseball and soccer teams in the New Bern area for more than a decade.

David is a recognized speaker on investments, financial planning, and taxes. He has written for and been quoted in numerous trade journals and mass media outlets, including *Money*, *Businessweek*, *U.S. News & World Report*, *The Wall Street Journal*, and other national and local publications. He was, for five years, the host of "All Things Money with David Blain," a weekly television and radio program. Under his leadership, BlueSky has received several awards and accolades throughout its history for their quality of advice, growth rate, and client satisfaction.

David resides in Trent Woods, North Carolina with his wife of twenty-three years, Caroline, and their five children.

ACKNOWLEDGMENTS

I owe a debt of gratitude to many people, most especially to my wife, Caroline, and my children Paul, Olivia, James, Patrick, and Kathleen; they are my "why" and keep me striving to excel. Also, I never would have made it this far without my colleagues from NAPFA who have served as my mastermind group throughout the years. And, of course, I need to thank the clients of BlueSky Wealth Advisors. Some of my most valuable learning experiences have occurred helping clients through their own life journey; without them, this book would not be possible.